NOT MY FATHER

UNDERSTANDING GOD'S NATURE IN THE MIDST OF
STORMS, DISASTERS, AND JUDGMENT

ROBERT GAY

Parsons Publishing House
Melbourne, Florida USA

Not My Father—Understanding God's Nature in the Midst of Storms, Disasters, and Judgment
by Robert Gay

Parsons Publishing House
P. O. Box 410063
Melbourne, FL 32941
www.ParsonsPublishingHouse.com
Info@ParsonsPublishingHouse.com

Publisher's Note: Publisher has opted to reference satan and related names with lowercase letters.

Cover Art: Micah Gay

ISBN-13: 978-1-60273-097-7
ISBN-10: 1-60273-097-0
Library of Congress Control Number: 2017960884
Printed in the United States of America.
For World-Wide Distribution.

DEDICATION

This book is dedicated to the following:

My wife, Stacey, whom I love dearly—Thank you for being there throughout the ups and downs of ministry. You have been a constant support and my biggest cheerleader. You are the best!

My children, Joshua, Kayla, and Micah, along with their spouses: Miranda, Kelvin, and Chelsea—You have made your daddy and mama proud. Your faithfulness to God and His call on your lives has brought great joy to our lives. Your children brighten my day—every single one of them: Josiah, Judah, Hannalee, Zoey, Levi, Gideon, Eliza, and Reagan. They are all such a blessing and have made me a happy "papa."

My parents, RL and Wanda Gay—You raised me in the way of the Lord, took me to church, and demonstrated to me the love of God. Your love and support have been unceasing through the years, and I will always remember the sacrifices you made for me.

Our church family, High Praise—Your faithfulness and dedication to the Lord is an example for others to follow. Thank you for your continued support. I love all of you.

TABLE OF CONTENTS

PREFACE

Man has always sought answers for things that he has not understood. Things that bewilder the minds of men trigger many questions. The questions of "why" and "who" have always been questions for which man has always wanted answered. These questions have been inexplicable at times. This has often driven man to create and fabricate conclusions rather than admit he did not possess the answer.

When the questions of "why" and "who" cannot be reasonably answered, speculation sets in. A speculation is an assumption that is made based upon the present thinking of the day. The understandings held at a given time within the church and the culture determine the stated speculation.

Speculations are usually based on opinions rather than direct evidence. Whenever there is direct evidence, it is considered a fact. We have heard this before when lawyers presenting evidence would argue the "facts of the case." Facts need no speculation; facts are real and concrete. They do not change. Facts are something that happened or are presently happening.

If I were to go outside and become saturated with water falling from the sky, I would not need to speculate that it was raining. There is factual evidence that rain is falling. I would be able to see it with my eyes, feel it on my body, and probably hear its effect with my ears. It would undoubtedly be raining.

Throughout the history of man, speculations have been made as to the origins of certain natural occurring events. Many of these speculations were the embryo of false religions and mythology. Man was attempting to explain something that lacked factual evidence. So, he made speculations as to the questions that everyone was asking: the questions of "why" and "who."

The unfortunate reality is there were continuous wrong answers to these questions. There was no fact basis, so assumptions were made. There was no evidence that linked a person directly to the event, so speculations were articulated.

The disposition many people took was that "when you don't understand, it must be God." God became the scapegoat for anything and everything that man experienced that was unexplainable. If it was disastrous, then God was definitely the culprit. Unfortunately, there are still many people who adhere to this disposition.

Much of Greek mythology stemmed from the need to explain certain things for which there was no explanation. There were all sorts of different "gods" who had power over certain elements of the earth and human existence. In Greek mythology, Poseidon was the god of the sea, storms, and earthquakes. He was the one that was responsible for these conditions.

If there was a storm, then Poseidon was responsible. If there was a hurricane or earthquake, then, you guessed it, Poseidon was responsible. Few people had enlightened understanding or spiritual insight of the natural elements, so they speculated that a supernatural power was responsible. Therefore, the Greeks created "gods" to be the answer to the questions that were asked regarding "why" and "who."

Regrettably, some of this same type of thinking has been present within the church. There are many who believe that God is the author of all storms. They believe God is in total control of all weather systems and that He sends storms, earthquakes, and other natural disasters. If it's bad and destructive, then God must be in the middle of it. My reply to these assumptions is: that's NOT MY FATHER!

Why do many believe this bad report about God? It is primarily because of speculation coupled with improper understanding of the character and nature of God. Their speculation is based upon natural events and weather that cannot be connected to individual responsibility. When there is no individual that can be held responsible, then God must be the One who did it. When the question of "who" is asked and there is no answer, then the default answer is "God."

Then there is the question of "why." If that cannot be definitively answered, then it is because of the sin of mankind. A person, a city, a people group, or the culmination of sin in an area has surpassed the threshold, and God is responding. Sin is the "why" and God is the "who." The belief is that the sin of the world is causing God to send storms and disasters as a means of judgment on the earth.

In this book, we will examine what the Bible specifically says concerning the issues of storms, disasters, and judgment. We will look at the very character and nature of God as it relates to these occurrences and events. I believe that this writing will enlighten you as to who God is and how He works within the earth. We will see how God interacts with naturally occurring weather events and disasters.

Throughout this book you will see the facts of God's Word. Speculation and opinion will be removed as we study the evidence that is contained throughout biblical history. God is faithful, and He is the same yesterday, today, and forever.

After you finish this read, if someone tells you that God sent a storm or disaster to your house, you will be able to say with me, "NOT MY FATHER!"

CHAPTER 1

WHAT DOES GOD HAVE TO SAY?

Hurricane Outbreak

In August of 2017, Hurricane Harvey, a category 5 storm, slammed into the Texas Gulf Coast. There was much damage from wind and rain in the southern Texas region. However, the greatest damage was that of historical flooding in the Houston area. Records were broken as this monster storm wreaked havoc throughout the region. Multiple thousands of people were left homeless, without water and food. Many escaped with only the clothes on their backs.

Just two weeks later, another major storm hit the Florida Keys and the Florida southwest coast. It was named Hurricane Irma. This storm affected the entire peninsula of Florida along with the northeast portion of the state. This included the Jacksonville region where certain areas also saw historical flooding.

Those who lived in the Florida Keys faced total devastation of property and the loss of power and water. Many throughout the state were forced to evacuate while others chose to do so voluntarily because of the strength of the storm. Many Floridians in the northeast region lost everything due to the degree and magnitude of the flooding. Homes and properties were destroyed which led many families to seek shelter. Others sought direction to know what to do in the wake of the hurricane.

About a week later, Hurricane Maria annihilated the island of Puerto Rico. This storm did unprecedented damage to the infrastructure of the island and left many without food and water. All were without electricity as the power grid was decimated. Roads were damaged and impassable.

In all these storms, both believers and unbelievers were affected. Those who love God and those who hate Him were affected in some way or another. Some experienced greater devastation than others. However, most everyone living in these regions was touched in some manner by these storms.

Questions and Statements of Origin

After the first storm, Hurricane Harvey, I began to hear people say different things about these storms. After Hurricane Irma, it only intensified. Then following Hurricane Maria, it was magnified yet again.

There was those who said that it was the judgment of God coming upon the Houston area for electing a homosexual mayor. Some said it was because of the compromise of the church. Others said it was because of certain church leaders in the area and region. Yet, there were other voices saying that these hurricanes came because of the proliferation of homosexuality in the different regions affected.

Then there were those that I heard declare it was the blessing of the Lord. They said God sent the storm, and it was His blessing. They expounded that when God sends these types of storms, they are always to bring blessing. It's interesting that those making these kinds of statements are not residents of the areas that were affected. Think about that.

There were yet others who said that these storms were a "sign of the times." They continued by saying these were indicators that Jesus was soon to come back, and the rapture of the church was imminent. These hurricanes were signifying that we are living in perilous times and that preparation was necessary.

There was yet another group of people who began to say that God was speaking through the storms. Since the first letters of each of the named storms spells HIM, surely God Himself must be involved and speaking through them. Furthermore, since there were three storms, they were indicators of the Godhead: Father, Son, and Holy Spirit. Some even connected these hurricanes to angelic visitations.

One other group of people began to say that these storms were sent to get the attention of the lost and unsaved. It was believed that God was using these hurricanes to bring people to a place of repentance. These storms were sent to bring about revival in the United States. Surely, amid all the devastation, peoples' hearts would begin to cry out to God for salvation and deliverance. After all, America needs to repent and turn to God (which I agree America does need to turn to God). It was communicated that God wanted to use these storms as an evangelistic tool for a great harvest of souls.

Good People Mistaken

These are just some of the things that I saw posted on Facebook™ pages and heard different people say. Some of these things were said by people that I both love and respect. However, good people can be wrong. That doesn't mean they are bad or evil, it just means that they are mistaken.

With so many different things being said, we know of a surety that someone is mistaken. We have all been mistaken at sometime in our lives, whether before salvation or after. We have all believed and said things that later we recanted or changed as our minds were renewed with the Word of God.

One of the first things that can readily be seen through all of these different perspectives is that there are many believers who begin to "spiritualize" hurricanes, storms, and disasters. They believe that God must be involved because of the magnitude of the devastation. Certainly, God must be in control of everything. Therefore, He is sending these storms and disasters. Right?

My Inquisition

When I first began to hear all these different perspectives articulated by different individuals within the body of Christ, I began to question myself since I respected the opinions of many of these people. I entertained for a moment that God might be sending judgment. After all, there is a tremendous amount of wickedness in the United States. However, I realized there were a lot of believers that were hurt during these storms. So, to believe that it was judgment, I would also be forced to believe that God would harm the righteous to punish the wicked. This was antithetical to the character and nature of God. We can see this in both the Old and New Testaments.

I also entertained the perspective that God was speaking something through these storms. Then, while reflecting on my understanding of the way God speaks today, I realized that God had already ordained ways that He communicated through His Word and by His Spirit. Hurricanes and storms were not God's divine methods of communication.

Let God Be True

I went through all these different perspectives and ultimately concluded that the only answer to the origination and reason of these storms was to be found in the Word of God. It could not be found in a feeling, sensing, vision, dream, or any other spiritual manifestation. I concluded that we must let God be true and every man a liar (Romans 3:4).

All these different voices saying different things caused me to search the Word of God, the Bible, to find out exactly what God had to say about hurricanes and storms. I had never done an exhaustive study on these things, so my position was not fully concrete. However, I did believe that God is a good God, that He is the giver of life, and we have authority to speak to storms, especially when our lives are in jeopardy. We will discuss this more in a later chapter. I did not believe that God would send hurricanes and tornados to destroy people and property.

The foundation of everything that we believe as Christians must be the Bible. The starting point for Christians must be that we believe the Bible is the infallible Word of God. If we fail to believe that, then we can go no further. If we fail to believe that, we cannot know that we are saved. If we fail to believe that, the rock upon which truth is built will become nothing but powder. This one truth must be securely fastened within our lives: **the Bible is God's infallible, unchangeable Word to us.**

Word and Spirit Agreement

While I believe that the ongoing work of the Holy Spirt is available for every believer today, we must understand that the Word and the Spirit always agree.

> This is He who came by water and blood—Jesus Christ; not only by water, but by water and blood. And it is the Spirit who bears witness, because the Spirit is truth. For there

> are three that bear witness in heaven: the Father, the Word, and the Holy Spirit; and these three are one. And there are three that bear witness on earth: the Spirit, the water, and the blood; and these three agree as one (1 John 5:6-8).

We see from this passage of Scripture that there is agreement in the Godhead. We see that the Holy Spirit is going to speak the same thing that Jesus speaks. The Holy Spirit will do the same thing that Jesus did. There is no disunity between the declaration of God's Word and what the Holy Spirit is speaking. The Bible is a more sure word of prophecy.

The things that we believe as Christians cannot be based solely upon what we feel or sense. Just because we feel something does not mean it's true. God has given us spiritual senses, but they are to operate within the boundaries and parameters of God's written Word. This is applicable for all the gifts of the Spirit.

Visions and Dreams

Equally, we cannot base what we believe on visions, dreams, and visitations. These are valid New Testament experiences, but they are not to be used to establish fundamental foundations of our faith.

> "But even if we, or an angel from heaven, preach any other gospel to you than what we have preached to you, let him be accursed" (Galatians 1:8).

Paul specifically declares that angelic visitations are not to be the basis of doctrine. He goes so far as to say, "Let him be accursed" if they are contrary to established biblical doctrine. These are very strong words. It helps us realize that angelic visitations and other spiritual experiences are not to be the foundation of what we believe. Paul was saying that if it doesn't line up with the gospel (the Word or the "good news"), then throw it away.

Biblically Illiterate

Many years ago, the Barna Group conducted a study and came to the conclusion that the church was "biblically illiterate." This is the unfortunate consequence of "feel good" sermons, youth pizza parties, and game nights, and nice socials while failing to preach the Bible. Since Christians, in general, are ignorant of biblical truth, they can be easily swayed with error.

There are far too many in the church today that are saying things that are not biblical. However, many just believe what they are told and never measure it against the truth of the Word of God. The gullible end up falling into the trap that the enemy sets for them through their own ignorance. They are led into captivity through the lack of knowledge. God said, "My people are destroyed for lack of knowledge" (Hosea 4:6).

The apostle Paul encouraged his spiritual son, Timothy, to study to show himself approved unto God and to rightly divide the word of truth. Paul knew that there would be those who would come into the church and promote various doctrines. His exhortation to Timothy was to "rightly divide" or correctly discern what was true.

The Measuring Stick

Anything that we believe as Christians should have its foundation and basis within the pages of the Bible. The Word of God is the measuring stick that we use to evaluate the truth and validity of anything that we may believe. If we cannot find it in the Bible, then we should depart from it. If it is not in agreement with the character and nature of the Father, then we should depart from it. Any other response would be falling short.

After considering all the different perspectives that people possessed concerning these recent hurricanes, the thought came to me that most people think nothing about a storm that does no damage and kills no one. However, a major hurricane that destroys everyone's property while killing people along the way has the fingerprints of God. I have three words for those who believe this: NOT MY FATHER.

This book is not only about storms, hurricanes, and disasters, but about the very character and nature of our Father. Is He the One who is sending storms to punish the people of the earth? Is He the One who is releasing catastrophes so people will know Him? Is this His way of speaking to people, both saved and unsaved? These are questions that we will tackle.

At the end of the day, my opinion is not the one that matters. However, what God says about the matter is what we need to hear.

I pray that you will put aside preconceptions and allow the Word of God and the Holy Spirit to illuminate the will of the Father. Allow His Word to come alive and hear His heart today.

CHAPTER 2

THE STILL SMALL VOICE

And Ahab told Jezebel all that Elijah had done, also how he had executed all the prophets with the sword. Then Jezebel sent a messenger to Elijah, saying, "So let the gods do to me, and more also, if I do not make your life as the life of one of them by tomorrow about this time." And when he saw that, he arose and ran for his life, and went to Beersheba, which belongs to Judah, and left his servant there. But he himself went a day's journey into the wilderness, and came and sat down under a broom tree. And he prayed that he might die, and said, "It is enough! Now, LORD, take my life, for I am no better than my fathers!" Then as he lay and slept under a broom tree, suddenly an angel touched him, and said to him, "Arise and eat." Then he looked, and there by his head was a cake baked on coals, and a jar of water. So he

> ate and drank, and lay down again. And the angel of the LORD came back the second time, and touched him, and said, "Arise and eat, because the journey is too great for you." So he arose, and ate and drank; and he went in the strength of that food forty days and forty nights as far as Horeb, the mountain of God. And there he went into a cave, and spent the night in that place; and behold, the word of the LORD came to him, and He said to him, "What are you doing here, Elijah?" So he said, "I have been very zealous for the LORD God of hosts; for the children of Israel have forsaken Your covenant, torn down Your altars, and killed Your prophets with the sword. I alone am left; and they seek to take my life" (1 Kings 19:1-10).

Elijah had just experienced a great victory at Mount Carmel. God had responded by fire and consumed Elijah's sacrifice while the prophets of Baal experienced no response from their false god. God had manifested His power before all of Israel and humiliated the false prophets simultaneously.

Elijah proceeded to order all the prophets of Baal to be captured and executed. Upon hearing of this mass execution, Jezebel threatened the life of Elijah. This threat from Jezebel caused Elijah to run and hide in a cave. It is at that place where God finds him.

In this moment of Elijah's despair and anger, God asks him, "What are you doing here?" Elijah responds by talking about his great zeal for God. He continues by saying that the entire nation of Israel had forsaken God's covenant, torn down His altars, killed the true prophets, and that they were now seeking to kill him, the ONLY servant of the Lord. To simplify this a little, Elijah said, "I'm great; they are awful and wicked."

After Elijah's condemning and judgmental answer regarding the nation of Israel coupled with self-pity and self-righteousness, God responds to him. He tells Elijah to stand on the mountain because He wants to reveal a truth to him. This is a truth that we need to receive today.

> Then He said, "Go out, and stand on the mountain before the LORD." And behold, the LORD passed by, and a great and strong wind tore into the mountains and broke the rocks in pieces before the LORD, but the LORD was not in the wind; and after the wind an earthquake, but the LORD was not in the earthquake; and after the earthquake a fire, but the LORD was not in the fire; and after the fire a still small voice. So it was, when Elijah heard it, that he wrapped his face in his mantle and went out and stood in the entrance of the cave. Suddenly a voice came to him, and said, "What are you doing here, Elijah?" And he said, "I have been very zealous for the LORD God of hosts; because the children of Israel have forsaken Your covenant, torn down Your altars, and killed Your prophets with the sword. I alone am left; and they seek to take my life." Then the LORD said to him: "Go, return on your way to the Wilderness of Damascus; and

> when you arrive, anoint Hazael as king over Syria. Also you shall anoint Jehu the son of Nimshi as king over Israel. And Elisha the son of Shaphat of Abel Meholah you shall anoint as prophet in your place. It shall be that whoever escapes the sword of Hazael, Jehu will kill; and whoever escapes the sword of Jehu, Elisha will kill. Yet I have reserved seven thousand in Israel, all whose knees have not bowed to Baal, and every mouth that has not kissed him" (1 Kings 19:11-18).

As you look at this at face value, it appears that God almost ignores everything Elijah is saying. We see God asking the same question of Elijah twice, "What are you doing here?" This question insinuates that Elijah was not supposed to be there. The question reveals that Elijah is not following the leading of the Lord at this time in his life. He is yielding to fleshly impulses such as fear, self-righteousness, and self-pity to name a few.

I believe when we closely examine this passage of Scripture, there are several principles that God is bringing to light. These are principles that when applied to our lives will help us rightly discern what God is doing and how He works with man. Just as God revealed this to Elijah, we need to see the same thing ourselves.

The Lord Was Not in the External

As you look at the previous Scripture passage, you will observe that God is emphatic about what He uses to speak and what He doesn't use. The Scripture declares,

"The Lord was not in the wind." Then it says, "The Lord was not in the earthquake." Then it states that "the Lord was not in the fire." The first thing to be noted is that God is not using natural occurring winds, earthquakes, and fires to speak to people.

Interestingly enough, these are some of the primary causes of natural disasters that we see today. God specifically declared that He does not attempt to speak through things like wind, earthquakes, and fires. His method of communicating is a "still small voice."

The Still Small Voice

The still small voice is the voice of the Holy Spirit on the inside of the believer today. When someone is saved and filled with the Holy Spirit, the voice of the Lord makes its abode on the inside of them. The indwelling presence of the Holy Spirit within them leads, guides, and directs them through life. This internal voice—the still small voice—is God's guidance system for the New Testament believer.

There is no need for God to speak to His people through storms and other disasters. If this were true, it would minimize the power and work of the Holy Spirit within the life of the believer. The need of storms for God to speak would in essence declare that the indwelling work of the Holy Spirit is insufficient. I do not believe this is the case.

Jesus spoke of the Comforter who would come after He ascended to the Father:

> And I will pray the Father, and He will give you another Helper, that He may abide with you forever—the Spirit of truth, whom the world cannot receive, because it neither sees Him nor knows Him; but you know Him, for He dwells with you and will be in you (John 14:16-17).

> However, when He, the Spirit of truth, has come, He will guide you into all truth; for He will not speak on His own authority, but whatever He hears He will speak; and He will tell you things to come. He will glorify Me, for He will take of what is Mine and declare it to you (John 16:13-14).

Notice that Jesus specifically says of the Holy Spirit that He would guide us. He went on to say that He would speak to us and show us things in our future. Furthermore, Jesus said that the Holy Spirt would glorify Him and impart to us what He (Jesus) possessed.

The bottom line is the agent responsible for the declaration and illumination of God's will, purpose, and plan is the indwelling presence of the Holy Spirit within the life of the believer. The Holy Spirit is the "still small voice" that guides Christians and reveals truth. He is the one that shows us things to come.

There is no indication in anything Jesus ever taught that God would use storms and disasters as a means to communicate with mankind. There is no indication that these things would be used to get the attention of the lost and backslidden. God's manner and method for speaking in the earth would be the voice of the Holy Spirit.

Spiritualization of Occurrences

It seems there are many people in the body of Christ that desire to "spiritualize" major weather occurrences. When there is a catastrophic storm or natural disaster, there are those who attempt to put a spiritual spin on the occurrence. They believe that God must be involved in some way or another. The greater the storm and disaster, the more they believe there is spiritual significance. They believe that storms could not merely be happening without the finger of God being somewhere in the midst.

I believe we should not attempt to spiritualize hurricanes, thunder storms, tornados, lightning strikes, earthquakes, and fires. It focuses attention on the external while God is working through the internal—that which we possess on the inside of us. Spiritualizing storms, hurricanes, and tornados sensationalizes naturally occurring weather events when God never designed this to be done.

The "spiritualization" of natural occurring weather events is usually done in an attempt to explain and make sense of something that is destructive in nature. It is done to put a positive spin on something that has produced destruction and chaos. Those who usually do this are well-meaning people. In their sincere desire to help comfort others, they believe there must be a spiritual explanation for what has taken place. However, sincerity does not guarantee accuracy or truth. The apostle Paul, before his conversion, was sincere when He was persecuting the church, but sincerely wrong in what he was doing.

Holy Spirit In Us, To Us, Through Us

When anyone attempts to make a prophetic word out of a storm or disaster, it is neither wise nor biblical. We will explain in more detail this principle as we continue this book. But first let me go back to the Scripture passage that involved Elijah. God was "not in the wind...not in the earthquake...not in the fire." The Lord was in the still small voice. The principle to be seen is that God does not send hurricanes, tornados, storms, earthquakes, fires, and disasters to speak; He uses the voice of Holy Spirit in us, to us, and through us!

God doesn't need a storm to speak through when His Spirit indwells you. He is there to speak to you and through you. The Holy Spirit is the revealer of truth, not storms and disasters.

Wilderness Walker or Canaan Conqueror?

When the children of Israel came out of Egypt, they tempted the Lord. This resulted in them wandering in the wilderness for forty years. While in the wilderness, they were led by a cloud by day and a fire by night. They were led by an external manifestations.

Once they entered into Canaan, there was no more cloud by day and fire by night. God signified that external manifestations were not the way that He would lead His people. Instead, He raised up Joshua as a leader. Later, God spoke through both the priests and the prophets. He spoke through those who had access to His voice.

Once the Israelites entered Canaan, they depended upon the leaders that God anointed with the Holy Spirit. They were the mouthpiece of God in the earth. God raised up priests and prophets to be his representatives; they had access to the still small voice. He still speaks to and through priests (the believer) and prophets (gift of the prophet).

As New Testament believers, we must understand that we are all priests unto God. We all possess the ability to hear the voice of the Lord. We DO NOT need to look to external manifestations to be led by the Holy Spirit. We do not look to storms and disasters as a means whereby God is communicating to His people.

The children of Israel were led by a cloud by day and a fire by night as they walked through the wilderness. You see, if we are looking to external manifestations to lead and guide us then we are functioning as wilderness walkers. However, if we are looking to those whom God has anointed and the Holy Spirit living on the inside of us to lead and guide, we are functioning as Canaan conquerors. Who would you rather be?

Elijah's Attitude of Condemnation

Looking back at the story of Elijah in the cave, we can see the prophet being condemning toward all of Israel. He actually says that he is the ONLY one who is still serving the Lord. God later sets the record straight and reveals that there are 7000 that had not bowed their knee to Baal.

As I studied this passage of Scripture once again, something leaped off the page that I had not seen before. For many years, I heard it taught that Elijah was wallowing in self-pity. That is an existing element clearly exhibited through his behavior. I had always looked at this entire passage of Scripture in the light of Elijah having a "pity-party" while complaining about his treatment. However, as I looked at it again, I began to see that Elijah was making an argument for God to bring judgment upon Israel. Think about it.

Think about what Elijah said. First, he said that he was "zealous" for the Lord. The Hebrew word used here means jealous and envious in a bad sense. It also means to provoke. He was declaring that he had been provoked by the behavior of the people. The reality is that Elijah was angry at the entire nation of Israel; he was upset in a major way.

The Case for Judgment

Elijah said all Israel had forsaken the covenant, torn down the altars of God, killed the prophets, and he was the only one in Israel serving God; he wanted to die himself. These all sound like reasons and justifications for God to "zap" Israel. After all, if Elijah was off the scene, there would be no others in Israel serving God (at least according to Elijah). This would give God the right and opportunity to pour out His judgment.

I have concluded it is very probable that Elijah was making an argument for judgment on the nation rather than merely conducting a pity-party. I believe this is the reason that God responded in the way He did.

God told Elijah to go and stand on the mountain. Then there was a great wind, then an earthquake, and then a fire. Could it be that God was revealing to Elijah that there would be no judgment through wind, earthquake, or fire? Could it be that God was signifying that He was not communicating through any wind, earthquake, or fire to judge Israel? I believe this is the reason.

Conviction

Instead, God began to speak through a still small voice. This is when Elijah covers his face. I've questioned before as to why Elijah covered his face. He had been carrying on a conversation with God and had not covered his face previously. What possessed him to cover up his face now?

Think about this. Could it be that Elijah is convicted about his judgmental and self-righteous attitude? Could it be that after God reveals that He is not going to send disasters to Israel that Elijah feels some degree of remorse? Could it be that his heart is pricked because of his "feel sorry for me" disposition that he took? Could it be he is convicted because of his fleshly behavior? Think about it.

God then sets the record straight with Elijah that there were thousands who were not Baal worshippers. This further reveals that God would not send any judgment because there were righteous people in the land (we will discuss this more later). God then tells Elijah to get on with his ministry by anointing specific ones whom He had called. Elijah's judgmental attitude and self-pity is being confronted by the Lord, and He brought it to an end.

I think it's interesting that many times those who call for judgment are the ones who end up convicted—convicted by the Holy Spirit. God is rich in mercy, not rich in judgment. When anyone begins to operate from a position of judgment, they operate contrary to the character of Jesus. When Jesus' disciples wanted to call down fire, Jesus rebuked them. He said they were operating in the wrong spirit. Jesus convicted them!

Voice of the Shepherd

> I am the good shepherd; and I know My sheep, and am known by My own. As the Father knows Me, even so I know the Father; and I lay down My life for the sheep. And other sheep I have which are not of this fold; them also I must bring, and they will hear My voice; and there will be one flock and one shepherd (John 10:14-16).

Jesus said that He is the good shepherd. He went on to say that His sheep hear His voice. It is the voice of the shepherd that sheep follow. It is the voice of the shepherd that leads and guides. It is the voice of the shepherd that gives direction so the sheep will continue following the correct path.

I continue to emphasize the voice of the shepherd. The voice of the shepherd is not storms and disasters. It is the same thing that Elijah experienced when he heard a "still small voice." It is the voice of the Lord speaking to the heart of man. It is the voice of Holy Spirit on the inside of us as He bears witness with our spirits that we are sons of God.

> "For as many as are led by the Spirit of God, these are sons of God" (Romans 8:14).

We could also read this Scripture in this manner: sons of God are led by the Spirit of God. Paul said that SONS ARE LED BY THE SPIRIT. Please hear this clearly; sons are not led by storms. As a son of God, I am to be led by the Holy Spirit. There is nowhere in the New Testament that insinuates in any way that we are to be led by storms or disasters. God leads us by His Spirit. God speaks to us by His Spirit.

It is important that we embrace the basic principle that **God speaks to us through the voice of His Spirit**. This is the manner that God has ordained for us to hear Him. He does not desire us to look to external things to find guidance. This is what those who practice astrology do. They look to the sun, moon, and stars to decipher what they believe to be celestial mysteries. This manner of seeking guidance is NOT MY FATHER!

CHAPTER 3

THE FALLEN WORLD

> Then to Adam He said, "Because you have heeded the voice of your wife, and have eaten from the tree of which I commanded you, saying, 'You shall not eat of it': Cursed is the ground for your sake; In toil you shall eat of it All the days of your life. Both thorns and thistles it shall bring forth for you, And you shall eat the herb of the field. In the sweat of your face you shall eat bread Till you return to the ground, For out of it you were taken; For dust you are, And to dust you shall return" (Genesis 3:17-19).

When God created Adam during the time of creation, He put him in a place of total perfection. There was no sin, sickness, disease, poverty, storms, or disasters. Adam lived in a garden that God created for him in Eden. The name "Eden" is derived from a word meaning pleasure.

Things were pleasurable in Eden. Every need Adam had was satisfied there.

God saw Adam was alone. He said it was not a good thing for man to be by himself. God caused a deep sleep to come upon Adam and took a rib from his side. With this rib from Adam, God formed woman. He brought this masterful creation to him, and they began to co-labor together.

Adam had been commanded to guard and protect the garden of Eden. This mandate was given to him before the woman was created. Adam's responsibility was to work in the garden and protect it (Genesis 2:15). He was to be the guardian of the garden.

The Turning Point

At some point in time, the serpent found his way into the garden and began dialoguing with Eve. While God had given Adam strict command to not eat of the Tree of the Knowledge of Good and Evil, the serpent deceived the woman, and she ate of the tree. Adam had failed to protect the garden, Eve had failed to heed the command, and then Adam disobeyed God by eating of the tree. Deception and sin entered the place that God commanded Adam to protect. Adam failed at his assignment; he missed the mark and thereby caused a major cataclysmic shift in the earth. We call this the fall of man. For mankind, it was sin's point of origination.

God came down in the cool of the evening to commune with Adam. Upon His arrival, Adam and Eve were nowhere to be found. They hid themselves and covered up because sin had produced the fruit of shame. Sin had caused the One who had fellowshipped and communed regularly with Adam and Eve to become a feared stranger.

The Consequences

After God heard what had taken place, He declared the consequence of their sin. He told the serpent that he would crawl on his belly. He furthermore said he would eat the dust of the earth and that the seed of the woman would bruise his head. God told the woman that she would experience pain in childbirth and that her husband would rule over her.

Lastly, God speaks to Adam concerning the consequences of his disobedience. The very first consequence was not directed toward Adam. The first negative sanction that God says is, "Cursed is the ground." We could also say it this way: cursed is the earth.

God made a declaration that the ground that Adam walked on, the earth, would be cursed. He continued by saying that it would require toil for Adam to be able to eat the fruit of the earth. Furthermore, God said that the earth would bring forth thorns and thistles.

The Shift

The fall of man produced a curse in the earth. That curse literally changed the very atmosphere of the planet. It set in motion a degradation from the perfection that was present at the time of creation. Things would no longer be perfect and without pain. The garden would no longer exist as it had previously. The earth's existence shifted.

Everything on the planet went from a place of perfect order to controlled chaos. While there were parameters in which things would operate, it was still a perversion of God's original creation. The fall of man released a consequence within the earth that we are unfortunately still experiencing today.

The reality is because of the sin of Adam, destruction and calamity entered the world. Sickness and disease that previously had no point of entry were ushered into the planet because of the fall. Poverty and insufficiency that formerly did not exist could now find way to manifest itself in a planet that was cursed. Anything you can name that is bad and destructive was given opportunity to manifest within the earth through the doorway of sin.

The Essential Link

You may be wondering why I would take time to rehearse creation and Adam's sin. It is because understanding the fall of man is essential to understanding storms and disasters that happen in the earth today. If you fail to understand the full ramifications of Adam's sin, you will seek to credit storms and disasters to some entity, whether it be God, the devil, judgment, blessing, etc.

This is the bottom line: **we live in a fallen world where there are natural occurring storms, tornados, earthquakes, and other disasters.** Now, that doesn't mean we are without protection and powerless. It just means that God is not sending them. They are a product of the curse that came on the earth.

We live in a fallen world. Unfortunately, there are different things that we must deal with and encounter. We regularly pull weeds because they grow where we don't want them. We sweat when we work because the sun, coupled with weather patterns, produce heat that causes our bodies to perspire. There are briers and thorns that exist on plants that produce beautiful flowers. We are required to wear gloves and be delicate with them or else we will get stuck.

All these things stated above are not attacks of the devil. Neither are they God. They are all products of the curse that came as the result of sin. God is not randomly causing thorns to come on your plants so that He can speak to you. The devil is not attacking because you perspired through your clothes while working outside in July with 95% humidity.

We must understand that there are things that happen because of living in a fallen world. These things will continue until there is a new heaven and a new earth.

Creation Groans

> For I consider that the sufferings of this present time are not worthy to be compared with the glory which shall be revealed in us. For the earnest expectation of the creation eagerly waits for the revealing of the sons of God. For the creation was subjected to futility, not willingly, but because of Him who subjected it in hope; because the creation itself also will be delivered from the bondage of corruption into the

> glorious liberty of the children of God. For we know that the whole creation groans and labors with birth pangs together until now. Not only that, but we also who have the firstfruits of the Spirit, even we ourselves groan within ourselves, eagerly waiting for the adoption, the redemption of our body (Romans 8:18-23).

Corruption and destruction were the result of the fall. Sin affected all of creation. Adam's sin caused the entire creation to be led into bondage. Now the earth groans while it awaits the manifestation of full redemption. This will happen when God ushers in a new heaven and new earth. But until then, there are things that we all must face and overcome.

Paul specifically spoke of sufferings in this passage of Scripture. This word "sufferings" means things undergone or hardship. Paul was referring to the experiences of living in a fallen world. There are things that human beings face as the result of sin in the earth. Both saved and unsaved face some of the same things. Natural weather occurrences including hurricanes, tornados, thunderstorms, and earthquakes are all a part of the experience of living in a fallen world. You can thank Adam when you see him in heaven. Welcome to earth.

Awaiting Full Redemption

I do not believe that in the beginning, when God created the heavens and the earth, that these types of destructive storms were in existence. These storms are the byproduct of sin's cataclysmic effect. Sin changed everything in the earth. The earth and all of creation now groans awaiting the manifestation of full redemption.

As those who have been redeemed by the blood of Jesus, we still await the full redemption of our bodies. While we are saved, we still live in a state of imperfection. Our bodies still age. Unfortunately, we will all grow old and die. This is not said to make one sad or melancholy; however, it is just the truth that has been in existence for thousands of years. This is what Paul said.

Until our bodies put on immortality it is subject to corruption. Likewise, until the earth experiences its full redemption, it is subject to storms and natural disasters. This does not mean that we are living as mere victims of Adam's fall. It does not mean there is nothing that we can do.

Afforded Protection Through Covenant

We are afforded protection and safety as we walk in a corrupted world. This is part of our covenant through the blood of Jesus. We can say like the psalmist David, "Though a thousand fall at my side and ten thousand at my right hand, it will not come near me" (Psalm 91).

Although sickness and disease were released into the world through the fall, we have a covenant of healing. Although poverty and lack were released as a byproduct of sin, we have a covenant of prosperity and blessing. Although destruction was released because of one man's sin, we have a covenant that contains the promise of protection and safety.

Jesus came to redeem all of mankind from the fall. He purchased us with his blood from the hold of satan. When His blood fell to the earth, He paid the price for the full redemption of the planet. We, as the church, are to enforce that redemption through preaching the gospel which results in lives changed and transformed. The church is on the earth to proclaim and enforce redemption through the power of the Holy Spirit working in our lives.

However, there are some things that will not be fully realized until the culmination of all things. One example of this is the full redemption of our body. Although the blood of Jesus purchased you completely (spirit, soul, and body), the full salvation of the body is reserved for the day of resurrection and translation.

I am purposely taking time with this because it is important to realize that God is not releasing destruction through storms any more than He is releasing sin, sickness, and poverty. All these things are products of the fall. However, we are afforded protection and safety in the middle of all these things. There is a day that is coming when there will be no more storms and disasters. However, that day is not yet.

The Sovereignty of God

There are many Christians who believe that God is fully sovereign and that God is in control of everything that happens within the earth. They believe that every storm, tornado, earthquake, and lightning strike is controlled by God. It is believed that God is orchestrating everything that happens on the planet.

If that were true, we would also have to assume that God is orchestrating every sin, murder, and vile thing that any person does. We would have to assume that God is randomly distributing sickness and disease to people. It would also have to be concluded that God arbitrarily chooses what territories, properties, and people would be destroyed through natural disasters.

To believe these things, it would be required to assert that we are all puppets and performers on a huge stage (the earth) where God acts as script writer and director. One would be forced to exclude the free will of man. One would have to conclude that we are here for nothing more than the entertainment of heaven. I will say this once again: that's NOT MY FATHER.

Understand that God has sovereignly given man a free will to make choices. Also, God has sovereignly initiated certain laws of nature. God does not make the choices for man; He advises man on the right choice to make, but does not make him choose rightly. Certain laws that govern the earth have been sovereignly put in place by God Almighty, but He is not actively orchestrating every weather event on the earth.

The Seasons of Life

After the great flood, God made a covenant with Noah. He promised that he would never destroy the earth through a flood again. He also told Noah this:

> "While the earth remains, seedtime and harvest, cold and heat, winter and summer, and day and night shall not cease" (Genesis 8:22).

God speaks to Noah of seasons. The interesting things about seasons is that each season has its own particular weather patterns. Your geographical location will determine the mildness or severity of those patterns. Some areas have a more severe summer than winter. Others have a more severe winter than summer. Every location has its own unique dynamics.

There are some areas that have very few storms while others will have many. Some areas are prone to tornados while others will never see one. Even tornados are more prone during certain seasons and weather conditions. Certain kinds of storms are associated with particular seasons and do not happen any other time of the year. The seasons are very important in the grand scheme of the earth and the survival of living organisms. Seedtime and harvest are in operation because of the seasons that exist.

Living in Florida

I was born and raised in Panama City, Florida located on the gulf coast of Florida. Being raised in northwest Florida, hurricanes were just a fact of life. They were a part of an ongoing weather pattern that had been in existence for hundreds and thousands of years.

I can remember as a young boy observing trash cans blowing down the street along with other debris during Hurricane Eloise that hit the west end of Panama City Beach. There was a tremendous amount of damage to our area from this storm.

Not one time did I ever hear anyone in our city say, "God must be sending judgement" or "God must be trying to say something to us" or "God is just blessing our city with a hurricane." We were smart enough to recognize that this was a natural weather pattern that was characteristic of our region. Those who lived there had chosen to do so knowing that hurricanes were a part of the package.

We had beautiful beaches, but ugly storms. We had gorgeous emerald green ocean water, but it would begin to churn and turn gray when the storms arrived. It was recognized that the beautiful and the ugly lived side by side. Similarly, God allows the righteous and the unrighteous to exist and live side by side. That's the reason we are commanded to be light in the midst of darkness. (We will talk more about this later.)

Living in Florida, we knew that between the months of August and October there was a greater chance of hurricane development. It was the middle of hurricane season. It was the season that brought with it the possibility of these storms. God was not sending them, it was merely the season.

Storms Happen

While God ordained the seasons, the storms within these seasons are the product of the fall of man. They are naturally occurring in the fact that they are produced by nature. Jesus spoke of the wise man and foolish man who both experienced the storm. However, the house of the wise man stood; he experienced no destruction. On the other hand, the foolish man experienced great loss.

It should also be noted that in the parable of the wise man and foolish man that Jesus never attributed the storm to His Father. Neither did He attribute it to the devil. Jesus did not attribute it to a blessing from heaven with a hidden message. I think that we can deduce from this parable that Jesus was saying, "Storms happen."

Living in a fallen world has brought about storms and disasters. God is not sending them, it's the direct and indirect result of Adam's sin. We must understand that there is protection afforded us, but the earth still awaits the manifestation of full redemption.

Our heavenly father loves and cares for us. We are the apple of His eye. Storms and natural disasters do not possess His fingerprints. They are not sent from heaven. God is not sending destruction and calamity. That's NOT MY FATHER.

CHAPTER 4

BIBLICAL RESPONSE: PROTECTION AND SAFETY

To hear some people talk, you would think that hurricanes just started happening in the last decade. It's as if these storms had never taken place before. Particularly when it's heard that God is now bringing judgment through hurricanes. However, they ignore that these storms have been taking place for hundreds and thousands of years.

It's amazing to me that the location of hurricanes and other types of storms still happen in the same geographical locations that they've been happening for years. It's not as if tornados changed the location of where they happen. Hurricanes didn't begin to take place in a totally different geographical area at a different time of the year. They still originate in the same areas and at the same time of the year. Again, as was stated previously, these are naturally occurring weather patterns.

Since much of the severe disastrous weather of late has been hurricanes, allow me a moment to share some facts about these storms:

- A hurricane is a tropical cyclone that naturally occurs.
- There are approximately 80 tropical cyclones a year.
- The strongest of these cyclones happen in the Pacific basin.
- There have been some storms that have killed close to a million people.
- Several storms have killed upwards of 100,000 people.

Tropical cyclones, like hurricanes, have been going on for hundreds of years. Many of the places that they affect were at one time uninhabited or sparsely inhabited. Therefore, there was limited destruction and fatalities, if any, from most of these storms.

Satellite weather tracking has only been available in the last 60 years. Therefore, many of the storms that took place were never known to exist unless mariners or airline pilots encountered them. One hundred years ago and beyond, the weather tracking was very archaic and it was difficult to predict coming storms. Unfortunately, this resulted in some of the highest death tolls involving storms because people were not able to prepare.

The bottom line is that there are no more hurricanes than what there has been before. These storms are not any stronger than they were hundreds of years ago. God did not suddenly release a rash of hurricanes in the earth to bring judgment on certain regions of America.

The people primarily affected by hurricanes are those who live in the regions where these storms have been known to exist. Those who live in Denver are not being affected by category 5 hurricanes. Likewise, those who live in Miami do not experience snow storms.

Believers and Unbelievers Together

When Hurricane Katrina hit New Orleans, there were some who said that it was God's judgment on the debauchery taking place in the French Quarter. Interestingly enough, the French Quarter wasn't damaged. The people who were affected were those who lived in a place that depended on the integrity of the levy system that held back Lake Pontchartrain. When the levies broke, they were flooded. These people did not live in the French Quarter. There were many believers that lived in these areas. Many people did not or could not evacuate. Unfortunately, many died. God did not do this. That's NOT MY FATHER.

God does not harm the righteous to punish the wicked. We will discuss this more in a later chapter. However, it's important for us to understand that God is not the author of hurricanes and these kinds of storms. These are indirectly caused by sin and the fall of man. Sin perverted the literal atmosphere and skewed God's original creation.

With this understanding concerning storms and disasters, we pose this question: "What is the biblical response to storms and disasters?" Since we know that these things happen, what should our response be as Christians? If it is truly God's judgment, then we should do nothing. If God is sending it, then we shouldn't pray nor speak to it as Jesus did. However, it is neither of the above, and the Bible has something to say concerning our response to these situations.

I believe that our response is to be four-fold. We will take time to discuss each one of these in detail. Allow me to list them for you first. These are correct biblical responses:

1. Pray for protection and safety
2. Speak to the storm
3. Evacuate and get away from it
4. Help those who are affected

We can find all these responses demonstrated in the Bible. Each of them happen in somewhat differing circumstances, but are the appropriate response in each given situation. It is important that we do what is appropriate at the right time. There may be times when you need to do all of the above.

Protection and Safety

Let's consider the first response: pray for protection and safety. I encourage you to read the following passage of Scripture in its entirety.

> Now when much time had been spent, and sailing was now dangerous because the Fast was

already over, Paul advised them, saying, "Men, I perceive that this voyage will end with disaster and much loss, not only of the cargo and ship, but also our lives." Nevertheless the centurion was more persuaded by the helmsman and the owner of the ship than by the things spoken by Paul. And because the harbor was not suitable to winter in, the majority advised to set sail from there also, if by any means they could reach Phoenix, a harbor of Crete opening toward the southwest and northwest, and winter there. When the south wind blew softly, supposing that they had obtained their desire, putting out to sea, they sailed close by Crete. But not long after, a tempestuous head wind arose, called Euroclydon *[a cyclone similar to a hurricane]* (Acts 27:9-14).

Now when neither sun nor stars appeared for many days, and no small tempest beat on us, all hope that we would be saved was finally given up. But after long abstinence from food, then Paul stood in the midst of them and said, "Men, you should have listened to me, and not have sailed from Crete and incurred this disaster and loss. And now I urge you to take heart, for there will be no loss of life among you, but only of the ship. For there stood by me this night an angel of the God to whom I belong and whom I serve, saying, 'Do not be afraid, Paul; you must be brought before Caesar; and indeed God has granted you all those who sail with you.' Therefore take heart, men, for I believe God that it will be just as it was told me. However, we must run aground on a certain island" (Acts 27:20-26).

And as day was about to dawn, Paul implored them all to take food, saying, "Today is the fourteenth day you have waited and continued without food, and eaten nothing. Therefore I urge you to take nourishment, for this is for your survival, since not a hair will fall from the head of any of you." And when he had said these things, he took bread and gave thanks to God in the presence of them all; and when he had broken it he began to eat. Then they were all encouraged, and also took food themselves. And in all we were two hundred and seventy-six persons on the ship. So when they had eaten enough, they lightened the ship and threw out the wheat into the sea. When it was day, they did not recognize the land; but they observed a bay with a beach, onto which they planned to run the ship if possible. And they let go the anchors and left them in the sea, meanwhile loosing the rudder ropes; and they hoisted the mainsail to the wind and made for shore. But striking a place where two seas met, they ran the ship aground; and the prow stuck fast and remained immovable, but the stern was being broken up by the violence of the waves. And the soldiers' plan was to kill the prisoners, lest any of them should swim away and escape. But the centurion, wanting to save Paul, kept them from their purpose, and commanded that those

> who could swim should jump overboard first and get to land, and the rest, some on boards and some on parts of the ship. And so it was that they all escaped safely to land (Acts 27:33-44).

We observe in this passage of Scripture a picture of supernatural protection. As believers, this is a part of our covenant. We are afforded protection and safety amid storms because of what Jesus did. Our salvation is not only redemption from sin and its power, but includes with it protection, wholeness, and safety.

Warning—I Perceive Disaster

There are numerous things that I would like to bring to your attention in this account. The first being that Paul was warned of an impending storm before the voyage was underway. He said, "Men, I perceive that this voyage will end with disaster and much loss." The Holy Spirit had revealed to him that there was danger awaiting them if they proceeded with their planned sailing.

Paul pleaded with the centurion in charge to postpone their trip. However, he was persuaded by the helmsman (captain) and the owner of the vessel. The centurion gave greater weight to those who were more seasoned in maritime voyages.

One of the principles to point out in this account is that **the Holy Spirit will warn us of dangerous situations.** Paul said that he perceived disaster. There was a check in Paul's spirit that it was not wise to set sail. We could even say that Paul received a word of wisdom concerning something that would take place if they proceeded.

It always pays to listen to the voice of the Holy Spirit. If you receive a check in your spirit concerning something that you are planning, you should at least take a step back and reconsider. We can avoid disaster and loss when we listen to the voice of the Lord.

Ultimately, the ship and all its cargo were lost. The only reason lives were saved was because Paul was on the ship and he had an assignment from heaven that had not been completed. The loss of property including the ship happened because those in authority failed to listen to God's anointed man.

I've seen people, when warned of impending disaster in their lives, fail to listen to warnings from anointed men and women. I've watched them continue down the road they were traveling and eventually experience great loss. It's very sad when this happens, especially when it could have been avoided.

Inside Information

If there is a sensing in your spirit that there is something you should avoid, then avoid it. If the Holy Spirit speaks to your heart that there is somewhere you shouldn't go, then don't go. Learn to be sensitive to the voice of Holy Spirit. As was said previously, this is the way that God leads His people. He leads us through the still small voice on the inside.

Paul was being led by the still small voice. The centurion, helmsman, and owner of the vessel were being led by external manifestations. Think about it!

The account declares that the south wind began to blow softly, and they thought they had gained their desire. They thought the conditions were favorable to set sail. However, Paul was being led by the Spirit and had INSIDE INFORMATION.

We see first-hand the dangers of being led by things that are manifesting externally. The owners of the ship put their trust in the way the wind was blowing. The wind was their source of information and revelation. Paul trusted the still small voice.

It is inside information that gives you the upper hand and allows you to circumvent dangerous situations. It is that inside information that God will use to help protect us and keep us out of harm's way. Don't be led by external manifestations. Be led by the Spirit!

Euroclydon

The Bible specifically says that after they set sail, they encountered a storm called Euroclydon. This is a storm that is defined and characterized by strong northeasterly winds. This is much like a hurricane or possibly a Noreaster. It is a tropical cyclone that forms in the Mediterranean Sea. Once again, these types of storms have been going on for hundreds of years.

These tropical cyclones, that we would call hurricanes, are rare meteorological phenomena. They are referred to sometimes as medicanes. They average less than two a year that form in the Mediterranean Sea. This is what Paul was facing—a rare occurring storm about which he warned everyone.

This was obviously no small storm. It beat the ship to the point that everything was thrown overboard while the ship was driven by the wind. They possessed no ability to set an established course; they were at the mercy of the storm.

The ship was battered by the storm to such a degree that they lost hope of any survival. They believed their fate was sealed and that they would all perish at sea. It was a very dire situation

The Answer Amid Crisis

Paul stands up and begins to speak to everyone on the ship. The first thing he says is, "You should have listened to me." In other words, he said, "I told you so." Paul reprimands them for not listening to him. He tells them they could have prevented the disastrous loss if they had listened to his counsel and never set sail.

Then Paul encourages everyone by declaring the word of the Lord that "there will be no loss of life." He went on to say that an angel of the Lord had stood by him and told him that God would protect everyone who was sailing with him. Although nothing changed immediately in their circumstance, they were assured of protection and safety. This was something they could cling to in the moment of crisis.

I believe God always has the answer in the moment of crisis. Our Father is mighty to save and deliver. The word of the Lord could have been that everyone would die except Paul. However, God who is rich in mercy, even when people failed to heed the prophetic warning from Paul, still saved and delivered them all.

Paul Didn't Say...

It is amazing to me how there are those in the church today who have no answer during situations of crisis and catastrophe. So, they will shout, "Judgment." They will declare, "Punishment." They will declare that God is involved in some way or another. However, Paul didn't do that.

As you look at this passage of Scripture, not one time will it be observed that Paul said that God had sent the storm to bring judgement. Not one time did he say that it was sent to teach them something. Not one time do we see Paul saying that God was attempting to say something through the storm. Not one time did He say God sent the storm because they failed to heed his warning. Paul warned them before the storm took place because God didn't desire them to experience it.

Word of Redemption

When God spoke through the angel in the middle of the storm, He spoke a WORD OF REDEMPTION. It was a word of protection and safety. It was a word of salvation and hope. There was no word of judgment after they were caught in the middle of the storm. During the storm, God spoke a word of assurance to those whose lives were in jeopardy.

It is also to be noted that Paul didn't say that it was the devil. He didn't credit it as a demonic attack against his ministry. I believe that if it had been demonic in nature he would have been more apt to stand up and rebuke it in the same manner that Jesus rebuked storms (we will discuss this in detail later).

I personally believe that Paul didn't have the authority to stand and rebuke the storm because the ones in authority had failed to heed the prophetic warning before they set sail. The failure to obey the word of the Lord had the consequence of loss. It wasn't the will of God. The Lord attempted to keep them from the loss through Paul's warning. However, they chose to ignore his word. Yet, God in His mercy still gave them a word of hope.

A Good Word for Bad People

It is so important that we as believers are those who bring a word of protection and safety when lives are in danger. We should be those with the word of healing to the sick and infirmed. We should be those with a word of blessing to those who are living under the curse.

Realize that the people that were sailing with Paul were not righteous people. There is no indication that this was a boat load of believers on a mission trip. This could not be compared to a ministry organized Caribbean cruise for believers to be refreshed. Paul was going to Rome bound and imprisoned. He was the only one who had a mission.

Most of the men on the ship with Paul were prisoners that were probably guilty of violent crimes. Many people would not even consider those passengers worthy of saving. Some of the authorities on the ship were ready to kill them all. However, Paul had a word of salvation in the middle of the storm.

Check Your Lens

I believe it's important for us as believers to check the lens through which we are looking. If you look through the lens of judgment and punishment, then every natural disaster will be perceived as that. If you look through the lens of God's mercy and love, then you will see a God who wants to save and deliver. Mercy triumphs over judgment (James 2:13).

If this same thing happened today, undoubtedly some believers would be questioning what Paul did wrong. Thoughts would be swirling in people's minds as to what kind of sin the apostle committed; he certainly did something wrong. After all, he was thrown in prison and then caught in a hurricane where he was saved by the skin of his teeth. God must be punishing him for some type of sin that he committed.

Truthfully, the will of God was that they were never to be in the storm. The ship was not supposed to set sail at that time. Paul had nothing to do with anything other than the saving of their lives.

I have come to believe that looking through the lens of judgment is worse than the sin for which people are being judged. The real sin is to look at everything though the lens of judgment and punishment. Jesus did not look at people through the lens of judgment. He looked at them through the lens of mercy, and we should do the same.

Looking through the lens of judgment will cause one's vision to be distorted. It will cause the picture to become an inaccurate representation of what is really taking place. It will result in a view of the Father as an angry God who delights and rejoices in punishing people. That's NOT MY FATHER!

God is not looking for a reason to bring judgment. Rather, He is looking for the opportunity to show His salvation. His desire is that we live under the protective umbrella afforded to us through the New Covenant. Protection and safety are benefits that belong to us. Therefore, we can pray and receive it in the name of Jesus.

CHAPTER 5

BIBLICAL RESPONSE: SPEAK TO IT

On the same day, when evening had come, He said to them, "Let us cross over to the other side." Now when they had left the multitude, they took Him along in the boat as He was. And other little boats were also with Him. And a great windstorm arose, and the waves beat into the boat, so that it was already filling. But He was in the stern, asleep on a pillow. And they awoke Him and said to Him, "Teacher, do You not care that we are perishing?" Then He arose and rebuked the wind, and said to the sea, "Peace, be still!" And the wind ceased and there was a great calm. But He said to them, "Why are you so fearful? How is it that you have no faith?" And they feared exceedingly, and said to one another, "Who can this be, that even the wind and the sea obey Him!" (Mark 4:35-41).

Let's consider the second biblical response to disasters: speak to it. In this account, there are just as many things that can be learned from what Jesus didn't say as from what He said. There were many different things that Jesus could have possibly spoken. I am sure He would have said them if it would have been applicable to the situation. Therefore, the manner in which Jesus addresses this storm gives us great insight to what we are to do and say as believers.

It's important to understand that Jesus was the will of the Father manifested in the earth. He said that the works that He did were the product of the Father working through Him. Jesus did nothing of His own accord; He was led by the Father in every dimension of His ministry.

God's Not the Originator

The first thing we must acknowledge is that Jesus did not say that God sent the storm. If this storm had come from the Father, it would have been wrong for Jesus to rebuke the wind and speak to the sea. It would be the same as Jesus rebuking Himself since He and the Father are unified. Jesus would have been rebuking the work of the Father if the storm had come from Him.

At one time in Jesus' ministry, while he walked the earth, He was accused by the Pharisees and religious leaders of casting out devils by the power of the devil. Jesus said that a kingdom divided against itself would not be able to stand. He said that a kingdom divided would come to desolation and an end. By this same principle, if the

Father was sending the wind and waves, Jesus would be destroying the kingdom of God by rebuking it.

The truth is that Jesus was merely in a boat that got caught in the middle of a storm. The truth is the Father did not send the storm. God was not attempting to set the stage so Jesus could demonstrate His authority and power. There were already plenty of manifestations of the devil where Jesus had opportunity to do that. Many sick and demonized people had already seen and experienced the power of God through the ministry of Jesus.

Don't Blame God

There are some who believe God allows bad things just so He can reveal His power. It is as if God creates evil so He can then show the triumph of good. While I believe that we overcome evil with good, the thought that God is sending the evil contradicts New Testament Scripture. The thought that God is sending the evil so He can demonstrate His power in antithetical to God's character and nature. That's NOT MY FATHER.

> "Don't blame God when you are tempted! God cannot be tempted by evil, and he doesn't use evil to tempt others" (James :13, CEV).

Notice the first statement in this verse of Scripture. Don't blame God! The Bible clearly says that God will not use evil to tempt (test or teach) any man. God has sent the Holy Spirit to be our teacher, not the devil or evil in the world. God is not in the practice of sending storms and disasters to see how you will respond. This is not His method or manner that He has laid out in His Word.

There is no indication in anything Jesus said when He was in the middle of the storm that the Father sent it to teach them some truth or principle. Nor did He say that the storm came to test their faith. Nor did He say that the Father wanted to communicate something through the storm. The storm revealed something (weak faith of the disciples), but did not teach them anything.

Not from the Devil

Another thing to note is that Jesus didn't attribute the storm to the devil. While He rebuked the wind, He didn't say that the devil had sent it. Many times, believers are far too quick in blaming the devil for any and all negative situations and circumstances within their lives. If something breaks, it's the devil. If there is an unexpected bill, it's the devil. If they stump their toe, it's the devil.

We must realize there are certain things that are just the product of living in a fallen world. Things break sometimes because we live in a world that experiences corruption; no eternal existence is in manifestation for anything naturally created. There are unexpected bills from time to time because of the things we choose to do and the economy that we are a part. The devil had nothing to do with us stumping our toe. It was either an accident, something was moved, or we failed to be cautious.

The truth is that sometimes people make poor decisions which result in negative consequences. These consequences neither come from God or the devil. To blame God is wrong. To blame the devil is equally wrong.

Many people accuse the devil of things in which he was never involved. These folks usually live their lives pointing the finger at whatever entity they believe is appropriate. The unfortunate reality is that their situations fail to improve because they never include themselves in the equation. Until we are willing to take responsibility for poor decisions and then change, we hinder the hand of God from moving in our lives.

Jesus Spoke to the Spirit

When Jesus dealt with things that were demonic in nature, He would speak to the spirit.

> Then they came to the other side of the sea, to the country of the Gadarenes. And when He had come out of the boat, immediately there met Him out of the tombs a man with an unclean spirit .
>
> When he saw Jesus from afar, he ran and worshiped Him. And he cried out with a loud voice and said, "What have I to do with You, Jesus, Son of the Most High God? I implore You by God that You do not torment me." For He said to him, "Come out of the man, unclean spirit!" Then He asked him, "What is your name?" And he answered, saying, "My name is Legion; for we are many" (Mark 5:1-2, 6-9).

> So all the demons begged Him, saying, "Send us to the swine, that we may enter them."And at once Jesus gave them permission. Then the unclean spirits went out and entered the swine (there were about two thousand); and·the herd ran violently down the steep place into the sea, and drowned in the sea (Mark 5:12-13).

It's interesting to note when this demonized man saw Jesus, he ran to worship Him. The demons controlling this man's life knew that Jesus possessed the power and authority to bring their "free ride" to an end. They began to ask why He had come to torment them. They recognized that Jesus had the ability to dispossess them of the home where they lived.

The conversation and dialogue that takes place is not between Jesus and a man. Rather, it is between Jesus and demons. Demons are spiritual entities under the control of satan who do his bidding. They follow satan's commands. Jesus spoke directly to the evil spirits. This was the way that Jesus dealt with situations that involved demons. He didn't speak to the man. This is a repeated pattern throughout the gospels.

Now, when Jesus encountered the storm, He didn't say, "I command you demon to come out of the wind." Why? It is because the wind wasn't controlled by the devil. Neither were the waves of the sea controlled by demons.

The type of thinking that links storms with direct demonic influence is skewed. While storms are the result of living in a fallen world riddled with sin, the devil is not actively involved in creating storms. This type of thinking lends itself to Greek mythology where there was a god of the sea, Poseidon, who had power to produce storms. We live by the Bible, not Greek mythology.

Jesus Rebuked the Wind

As you read the account of Jesus in the boat, it is clearly seen that Jesus REBUKED THE WIND. He didn't rebuke a demon. Jesus spoke directly to the wind. If it had been demonic, He would have spoken to the demon.

The word "rebuke" means to censure, admonish, and forbid. Jesus, by His faith, prohibited the wind to continue to blow. He released words of faith that caused the wind to stop. Wow! When He did this, the disciples were amazed. Jesus then reprimanded His disciples for the lack of faith. I believe that He was rebuking them for several things.

The first thing I believe Jesus was reprimanding them for was their own belief that He didn't care about them. They woke Him up out of the middle of a nap with an accusation that He was uncaring. I don't believe that Jesus appreciated them waking Him up in that manner. This was a manifestation of unbelief.

The second reason that Jesus rebuked them was their statement that they were perishing. That means that they believed they were all going to die. Jesus had said to them previously, "Let us cross over to the other side." Believing those words alone would have brought assurance of their safety.

The third reason Jesus reprimanded them was because of their fearfulness. Fear had gripped their heart and they were in a state of panic. They wanted Jesus to do something about the situation rather than use the authority He had already given them. They placed the responsibility on the shoulders of Jesus rather than take responsibility themselves.

Jesus asked them, "Why is it you have no faith?" Jesus expected more out of them than what they demonstrated at that moment. He was curious as to why they did not believe. He could not understand why they were reacting to adversity in this manner. They had seen His miracles; they had seen supernatural manifestations. Why were they so fearful and unbelieving?

Jesus' Example

Jesus demonstrated what they should have done; He rebuked the wind. He spoke to it and released His faith through the words of His mouth. As He did this, nature responded: the wind stopped blowing.

Jesus set an example for you and I to follow. He was the will of God manifested in the earth. That means this: if Jesus spoke to the storm, then we can speak to the storm. If He commanded the wind to stop then we can too! If He commanded the sea to stop raging, it is possible for us to do the same.

I know there are many people who say, "That's over the edge." However, Jesus said we would do the works that He did and even greater! That's right. Jesus said we would rebuke storms, too! WOW!

Speak to the Mountain

I've exhorted our church body that we need to speak to the mountain rather than talk about it. That's what Jesus said. He said to speak to the mountain. Well, if we can speak to the mountain then we can speak to the storm. We should speak to the storm rather than talk about it.

It's always been amazing to me at the number of people who, when there is a report of a storm, hope the storm comes their direction. They begin to expect the storm to come their way. They talk about the thing rather than speak to it.

Jesus spoke to the waves of the sea. He said, "Peace, be still." In the midst of turmoil Jesus spoke, "Peace." He didn't get out on the bow of the boat and say, "Wow, these are some huge waves." Jesus called those things which were not in existence as though they were. We should do the same!

Jesus exampled speaking to the storm. He didn't example talking about it. If we will do what Jesus did, we will have the same results. We have been given His power and authority. Let's use it!

Praying Storms Away

When some hear the news that a storm is headed their direction, they begin to pray that God would send it to some other geographical location. Many times, it involves a place where there is a populous of people. So, in essence they are praying that someone else would be affected rather than them.

Jesus never said to pray storms on others. Neither did He example this in His life. Jesus spoke the word so that the storm would be dissolved and dispelled.

Any type of intercessory prayer should focus on the disempowerment of the weather system. It should focus on protection and safety for all. It should never be for the track of it to be shifted and others be hurt. We should never pray or "wish" any potential destructive storm system to go somewhere where others could be harmed. This borders on the practice of "witchcraft" prayers.

Some have prayed that God would send disasters to places where they felt there was concentrated wickedness. They believe many times that this is justifiable because of the degree of unrighteousness present. They even use the account of Jesus casting demons into pigs as an argument to legitimize this type of prayer.

Jesus did cast demons out and allowed them to go into pigs. However, it was unlawful for Jews to eat pork. It was an unclean animal. They should not have been raising the pigs. Jesus cast demons into an animal that was contraband for the nation of Israel. It would be the equivalent today of a drug raid and then burning the captured contraband. This is a good thing! There is no comparison of what Jesus did by casting out demons into pigs to that of someone praying a storm would go to an area or region that they considered wicked. Praying or wishing storms and disasters on anyone is not right or biblical. That is NOT MY FATHER!

Speak Words of Faith

When we hear news of a damaging weather system coming our direction, we should respond by speaking words of faith. That would include words of safety, protection, and assurance. It would also include words spoken to the storm to dissolve and dissipate. Declare that the storm will weaken.

We must understand that we have been given power and authority through the name of Jesus. We can speak, release our faith, and see things change. Jesus exampled it before us. He spoke to the storm and it subsided. If we will do what Jesus did, we will see the same results.

CHAPTER 6

BIBLICAL RESPONSE: EVACUATE

> Then it came to pass the seventh time, that he said, "There is a cloud, as small as a man's hand, rising out of the sea!" So he said, "Go up, say to Ahab, 'Prepare your chariot, and go down before the rain stops you.'" Now it happened in the meantime that the sky became black with clouds and wind, and there was a heavy rain. So Ahab rode away and went to Jezreel. Then the hand of the LORD came upon Elijah; and he girded up his loins and ran ahead of Ahab to the entrance of Jezreel (1 Kings 18:44-46).

Let's look at the third biblical response to disasters: evacuate. After three and a half years of famine, Elijah declares that a storm is coming. Elijah possesses spiritual revelation that a storm is brewing. He has inside information of things that are forthcoming. He tells Ahab to get his chariot ready and go home. Otherwise, the rain will stop him.

Elijah basically tells Ahab, "Run!" In this passage of Scripture, we witness Elijah telling Ahab to evacuate. Not only does he admonish Ahab to do so, but Elijah evacuates, also.

We read that the hand of the Lord comes upon Elijah for the purpose of running ahead of a weather system. Under the anointing of the Holy Spirit, Elijah beat Ahab to Jezreel. Even though this was not a destructive storm, God still moved upon Elijah to get out of the way and find a place of refuge.

Get Out of the Rain

One of the things we see specifically in this account is that there are times when the appropriate thing to do is evacuate ahead of a storm. I would venture to say that God may instruct someone to evacuate. Through the voice of Elijah, God instructed Ahab to do so. Likewise, this caused Elijah to do the same.

There are times that evacuating and leaving an area or region which may be threatened is the right thing to do. There is no need for someone to go through a horrendous storm if it can be avoided. There is no reason for a family to sit in the dark for weeks when it could have been avoided by evacuating.

There is no set rule for when you should or shouldn't leave a region that is threatened. I believe it's important to be led by the Holy Spirit. I believe He will instruct you with the correct strategy in every situation. I also believe it would be wise to heed the warnings of authorities in the area or region. If they say, "Evacuate," then you should leave. There is no need to prove to anyone the measure of your faith by remaining in a threatening situation.

Get Out of Town

In October of 1995, I had just returned home from a ministry trip. While my family joined me on the majority of ministry engagements, I had traveled to the West Coast, and they were unable to join me. When I got home, my wife informed me there was a hurricane in the Gulf of Mexico that the local meteorologists were watching closely. The name of the storm was Hurricane Opal.

We went to bed that evening with the storm being a Category 2 hurricane. It was not expected to threaten our immediate area. I woke up around 4:00 a.m. and turned on the television. Opal had escalated to a strong Category 4 hurricane overnight. It had also shifted its course and was said to be on a direct path to hit the Bay County area which was where we lived.

We only lived four blocks from the bay. We didn't realize at the time, but we were in a place that could be flooded if there was a strong storm surge. A six-foot storm surge would cause water from the Bay to come into our yard and possibly our home.

Once I saw how the hurricane had strengthened, I woke up my wife, Stacey, and told her, "We need to evacuate." At that time, we had three children. Our oldest son, Joshua, was ten years old, our daughter, Kayla, was six years old, and our youngest son, Micah, was just three years old. As my wife and I discussed this, we concluded that there was no reason for us to stay at our house and subject our family to all the different possibilities that the hurricane might bring. We decided to believe for the best and prepare for the worst. That meant evacuation.

Both my wife and I were born and raised in Panama City, Florida. My family had never evacuated for any storm. Her family had only evacuated for one storm: Hurricane Eloise in 1975 when she was twelve years old. I had personally seen damage from hurricanes, but had never experienced any myself. We were accustomed to riding out these storms.

However, when I woke up that morning, I had a sensing that we needed to evacuate. We immediately began to pack and get things ready to leave. We also prepared things around the house and secured things outside the house. We decided that we would drive to Orlando because of the path of the storm. That would keep us out of its fury and not be susceptible to its wind and rain.

We arrived in Orlando that evening and checked into a hotel. We planned on staying for three to four days. The next day, we took our kids to Disney World and had a wonderful time as a family.

Meanwhile, back in Panama City, the area was hammered by strong winds and rain. Power was knocked out throughout the area. There were houses directly on the beach that were swept out to sea. A tremendous amount of damage was realized throughout the region. As a result, there was a "no travel order" mandated. No one was allowed to come into the city for several days.

If we had stayed home, we would have been without power for several days. Our children would have experienced howling winds and rain for hours. It would not have been a pleasurable experience. Instead, we had fun together in Disney World. I believe we made the correct decision and were led by the Holy Spirit to evacuate.

Follow After Peace

Understand this, we did not evacuate because we were afraid for our lives. Fear was not the motivating factor in our actions. We believed that this was the best thing for us to do in the given situation. This is what we had peace about doing. We were following the road that produced peace in our hearts.

Evacuating before a storm does not mean that you are afraid. It also doesn't mean that you have no faith. It doesn't declare that you have failed in speaking to the storm. It does not mean any of these things whatsoever.

No one has to prove that they are full of faith by standing on the beach waiting for a hurricane to hit. That's not faith; that's foolishness. You can speak to a storm while being hundreds of miles away from it. You don't have to be in the eye of a hurricane to use your faith. Evacuating is not the equivalent of raising the white flag of surrender to the fury of a hurricane or any storm.

Common Sense

Evacuating in some situations is the byproduct of using the brain that God has placed in our heads. If it's pouring down rain outside, we have enough sense to get out of the rain. Using common sense does not discount the walk of faith. It only excludes the practice of foolishness in the name of faith.

I don't know of any man alive today that operated in greater faith than Elijah. He was a man of great faith and spiritual insight. However, when he saw there was a storm coming, he evacuated. Elijah walked in faith, but not foolishness or presumption.

There are many that die in severe storms needlessly. Most of these people die because they refuse to evacuate and leave the area. They didn't die because it was "their time." They died because they didn't get out in time. Refraining from evacuating when a disastrous storm is threatening will prove nothing. It does not prove that someone is fearless or full of faith. One should never put their life in jeopardy in the name of faith.

Protection While Absent

When we evacuated in 1995 for hurricane Opal, we made declarations over our property. We declared supernatural protection over our home. We commissioned the angels of the Lord to be about our home while we were absent.

We were already accustomed to doing that since we traveled in ministry frequently.

When we were finally allowed to come back into the city (about three days following the storm), we drove into our neighborhood. There were houses with shingles blown off and roof damage. Trees were blown down and all sorts of other damage existed on our street and in our neighborhood. As we drove up in the driveway of our home, we were joyfully surprised. Not one shingle blew off our house. There were no trees down. There was absolutely no damage to our home or property. It looked as if someone had blown the leaves from the yard and it had just been manicured. We were amazed.

The only thing that happened was the trampoline in the backyard was blown from one end of the yard to the other and was propped up on the fence. Our neighbor, who remained at his house during the storm, told me that it looked like a tornado came through, lifted the trampoline, and then gently placed it along the fence.

Our faith was still at work the entire time that we were away. Our property was not touched; our things were protected. The angels of the Lord had encamped about us and protected both our family and our stuff. God was faithful to do what He promised He would do.

CHAPTER 7

BIBLICAL RESPONSE: HELP AND AID

> Then one of them, named Agabus, stood up and showed by the Spirit that there was going to be a great famine throughout all the world, which also happened in the days of Claudius Caesar. Then the disciples, each according to his ability, determined to send relief to the brethren dwelling in Judea. This they also did, and sent it to the elders by the hands of Barnabas and Saul (Acts 11:28-30).

God Revealed vs God Sent

Let's consider the fourth biblical response to disasters: providing help and aid by the Spirit. Notice that the Holy Spirit revealed there would be famine. It does not say that God was sending the famine. It says that Agabus prophesied that a famine was coming that would affect people.

It is important to understand when a prophet reveals something by the Holy Spirit which is to happen, it does not necessarily mean that God is involved in its origination. It doesn't mean that God is doing it or sending it solely because it is prophesied. God will show us things to come through the voice of the Holy Spirit. However, everything revealed does not implicate the Father God in its origin.

When the Holy Spirit revealed that there would be a famine, God was warning the people of something that was to come. There is no indication that this famine was a judgment. There is also no indication that it was an attack of the devil. There is no indication that God was attempting to communicate something through the famine.

God Speaks to Prepare

God was actually speaking and communicating through the prophet, Agabus. May I say that God was communicating very clearly? He didn't need to speak through a famine. God was giving them inside information so they could appropriately prepare and be a channel of provision.

This is much like what happened with Joseph who interpreted a dream that Pharaoh dreamed. The interpretation of the dream was that there would be seven fat years followed by seven years of famine. God used Joseph to enable the nation of Egypt to prepare for the impending famine. As a result, Joseph's family was saved.

Understand this principle: **God reveals things that will happen to provide salvation for those who are in danger.** He doesn't reveal these things (natural weather occurrences) as unavoidable, doomsday, apocalyptic happenings with no hope of salvation or safety. That's NOT MY FATHER!

Redemption at the Foundation

We see in both the Old Testament and New Testament that God uses the prophetic ministry to forewarn of an impending natural disaster so that provision can be made and lives will be saved. This is the reason God used Agabus to announce this famine. God wasn't releasing a famine through the prophetic ministry; God was saving people from famine through the prophetic ministry.

It's important that at the foundation of our revelation of the character of God be the understanding that **God is redemptive in what He does.** God's Word is redemptive. His Spirit is redemptive. His actions are redemptive. He is not seeking to destroy. Rather, He is seeking to redeem and restore. Those who fail to embrace this understanding will look at things through the incorrect lens.

Compassion in Crisis

After Agabus delivers the word of the Lord to the disciples, the Bible declares that they determined to send relief to the brethren in Judea and so they did. They knew there were those who needed help. They allowed the compassion of the Lord to motivate them to action.

Only when passion gets legs and walks does it become compassion. The disciples realized that the prophetic word released was not ministered just so they would have inside information. It was released so they would be motivated to do something. This word was a call to action; these disciples sent aid.

When Hurricane Harvey wreaked devastation throughout southeast Texas, we received an offering in our church body. We sent that offering to aid those bringing relief to believers in these areas that were affected by flooding. We helped by sending new shoes to those who needed them. So many people experienced great loss, and they needed help.

During this time, there were those who were prophesying and declaring that this was God's judgment. Others were saying that it was a sign of the times. Most of them did not live in the areas affected and most of them did nothing to help.

If God actually sent Hurricane Harvey as a judgment, then anyone who sent aid would be thwarting the purpose of God. After all, if God is judging them, who are we to help them escape what God is sending? We should just let them suffer if God is sending it. Please hear this: that's NOT MY FATHER!

Likewise, if God sent the famine about which Agabus prophesied, then they should have done nothing. If God sent it, they circumvented the purpose of God by sending aid. Why should we attempt to get people out of what God is sending? Can you see the fallacy of this kind of thinking that God sends disasters?

The Prophetic and Storms

During some of the hurricanes of 2017, there were those attempting to figure out why these storms were happening. Is God attempting to tell us something? What does all of this mean? Some said there was certainly a prophetic message within all these storms.

I understand that three major hurricanes having affected the United States territories all within a one-month time frame can cause people to question. However, jumping to conclusions based upon external appearances will cause error. We must go to the Bible and rightly divide the Word of truth to come to accurate conclusions.

To say there are prophetic statements being made through storms that are killing people and destroying property is certainly an assumption that is not biblical. It's hard to fathom that someone would say disastrous hurricanes and prophetic ministry are synonymous. That's NOT MY FATHER!

Nothing New

Thinking like this can be traced back to the days that Jesus walked the earth. It was even in His own disciples. They were not bad men. They loved Jesus, but their thinking was skewed.

> Now as Jesus passed by, He saw a man who was blind from birth. And His disciples asked Him, saying, "Rabbi, who sinned, this man or his parents, that he was born blind?" Jesus answered, "Neither this man nor his parents sinned, but that the works of God should be revealed in him. I must work the works of Him who sent Me while it is day; the night is coming when no one can work. As long as I am in the world, I am the light of the world." When He had said these things, He spat on the ground and made clay with the saliva; and He anointed the eyes of the blind man with the clay. And He said to him, "Go, wash in the pool of Siloam" (which is translated, Sent). So he went and washed, and came back seeing (John 9:1-7).

In this account, as Jesus passes by a man who was blind from birth, His disciples ask Him a question. They ask Him, "Who sinned, this man or his parents, that he was born blind?" The disciples believe that either the blind man or his parents were responsible for the man's blindness. They believe that someone had to sin. They believe that he is blind as a result of his sin or his parent's sin.

This is much like some today. They ask, "Who sinned that this storm has brought disaster on that city?" They ask the question and then answer it with their own understanding. They believe that any natural disaster must be directly due to someone's sin. Something must be going on within the area and the region that made it susceptible to this kind of disastrous event.

Jesus answers the question posed by His disciples. He answers, "Neither this man nor his parents sinned." Jesus said that this man was not blind as a direct result of his sin or his parents sin. If sin itself had caused the blindness, then all the disciples would have been blind, too. Think about it. They had all sinned.

Likewise, I believe the same answer is applicable to those who are asking the questions as to what's going on to cause these hurricanes. In the words of Jesus, "Neither this man nor his parents have sinned." There is no particular sin that is causing hurricanes and storms.

Asking Questions or Demonstrating Answers?

The problem we have is that people are asking the wrong questions. Instead of asking, "Why?" they should be asking, "How can I help?". Instead of asking, "Who sinned?" they should be asking, "What can I do?".

This is what Jesus did. After answering the question posed by His disciples, He said, "The works of God should be revealed in him" and "I must work the works of Him who sent me." Jesus was actually saying to His disciples that the question of "Why" was not relevant. Religious arguing, debating, and pointing of the finger was not going to cause the blind man to receive his sight. Jesus said to forget about why and get to work. He said to do something.

So, Jesus healed the blind man rather than debate as to who had sinned. He wasn't called to debate doctrine. Jesus was called to reveal the will of the Father and bring healing and deliverance to people. While His disciples were asking the irrelevant question of "why," Jesus was revealing the power and anointing of God by healing the blind man. Jesus spent His time revealing the answer rather than asking the question.

While many people are attempting to figure out things that occur and continue asking the wrong questions, there are people who will be like Jesus and do something. You can choose to be like Jesus' disciples and ask irrelevant questions, or you can be a person moved with compassion. We can be those who are the answer or those who always ask the questions. Which do you want to be? Who would you rather see if you were in need?

Let us be the ones with the answer. We are called to bring healing and help to those in need. We are called to be the light amid darkness. We are called to demonstrate the answer.

CHAPTER 8

THE FLOOD AND JUDGMENT

The first principle to understand in talking about natural disasters and its connection to judgment is this: **God will not harm the righteous in order to judge or punish the wicked.** It is important that this biblical principle be at the foundation of our understanding. This is a recurring principle that is demonstrated throughout the Bible. It is seen in both the Old and New Testaments.

Many times, when there is a disastrous event that occurs, we may hear some say that God sent it to judge an area or region. Those who say this are actually declaring that God is judging the people within that region. The problem with those statements is that there are righteous people living in the areas being affected.

When someone says that God is sending judgment on an area while righteous people are living there, they are actually accusing God of punishing the righteous along with the wicked. Even Abraham recognized that God would not do this (will discuss later). I would like to shout this out: that's NOT MY FATHER!

Responsibility and Accountability

I grew up in a family of four: my parents, my brother and myself. My parents believed that they were given the responsibility to train their children in the way of the Lord which included discipline and punishment if we disobeyed. Yes, my father and mother did not spare the rod.

However, I did not receive the punishment for my brother's disobedience. Neither did he receive a spanking for my disobedience. Can you imagine parents that would line up all their children and levy punishment on all of them for the disobedience of one? That would be unrighteous.

My parents required each of us to be accountable for our own actions. We each received the reward for our own behavior. My daddy did not discipline me for what my brother did or vice-versa. My parents loved both me and my brother, and they taught us to accept responsibility for our own actions.

There are some who believe that God will destroy a region and a territory through a hurricane or tornado while there are still thousands and even millions of believers living there. Therefore, they credit God with sending monster storms to destroy and demolish. They say that God's fingerprint is in the middle of what is transpiring. However, I will say once again: that's NOT MY FATHER!

Righteous Judgment

The New Testament has some things to say about judgment. Although we will not cover everything it says concerning the topic, we must understand that there is a "righteous judgment" of God (Romans 2:5). However, that judgment (condemnation and punishment) is not to be shared with the righteous.

The righteous judgment of God is never intended to be experienced by the redeemed of the Lord. We were redeemed from judgment. Jesus took our judgment on the cross. It would be unrighteous for God to send judgment on us since Jesus bore the judgment that we deserved. To say that God sends judgment on the believer, nullifies the power of the cross and the blood of Jesus.

Power in the Blood

We see a picture of judgment in the final plague of Egypt. God caused the angel of death to visit every household throughout the land of Egypt. Every firstborn male child throughout the land died in one night. However, he told the Israelites to make a blood sacrifice, a spotless lamb. He furthermore instructed them to take the blood of the lamb and sprinkle it on the doorposts of their houses. Then God said this:

> "Now the blood shall be a sign for you on the houses where you are. And when I see the blood, I will pass over

> you; and the plague shall not be on you to destroy you when I strike the land of Egypt" (Exodus 12:13).

Every time I read this Scripture, my heart leaps! God said that the blood of the lamb would cause the plague (judgment) to pass over and not harm them. This was the blood of a natural lamb, an animal that grazes in the field. If the blood of an animal would cause the judgment (plague) to not touch them, how much more will the blood of Jesus cause judgment to be far from us. Jesus' blood is the anti-judgment agent.

Those in the body of Christ should not be the first to cry out, "Judgement!" We should be the first to cry out, "Redemption!" We should be the first to say that our Father is not sending judgment on the earth to punish everyone including the righteous.

We must understand that for God to bring judgment through natural weather occurrences where the righteous are affected is inconsistent with the character and nature of God. We do not observe in the Bible that God randomly and arbitrarily sends judgment and punishment on people. He particularly does not do this when there are righteous people living in the region. The only way this would happen is if God gives the righteous a way to escape (will discuss more in detail later).

Jesus said this:

> "Behold, I send you out as sheep in the midst of wolves. Therefore be wise as serpents and harmless as doves" (Matthew 10:16).

Notice the words, "I send you." Jesus said that He sent us as sheep in the middle of wolves. So, He has planted us in the world right in the middle of evil and wickedness. With that in mind, the question I have is this: if God sends us into the place of evil and wickedness, why would He then pour out judgment on the places that He sends us and cause us to reap the punishment for the sin of others? This would be the equivalent of an army commander sending troops into an area to only kill those troops if things didn't immediately improve. What kind of commander would that be? One that needed his post taken away from him for sure.

So what kind of God would we be serving that would send us as sheep among wolves to only decide to bring judgment on the sheep and the wolves together? Once again, that's NOT MY FATHER!

We are called to be light in the middle of darkness. We are commissioned as sheep in the middle of a pack of wolves. Jesus said we are to be the salt of the earth. Salt is used to season and preserve (bring salvation). We are not here on earth so judgment can come. Rather, we are here so salvation and blessing can be released!

> For if God did not spare the angels who sinned, but cast them down to hell and delivered them into chains of darkness, to be reserved for judgment; and did not spare the ancient world, but saved Noah, one of eight people, a preacher of righteousness, bringing in the flood on the world of the ungodly; and turning the cities of Sodom and Gomorrah into ashes, condemned

> them to destruction, making them an example to those who afterward would live ungodly; and delivered righteous Lot, who was oppressed by the filthy conduct of the wicked (for that righteous man, dwelling among them, tormented his righteous soul from day to day by seeing and hearing their lawless deeds)—then the Lord knows how to deliver the godly out of temptations and to reserve the unjust under punishment for the day of judgment (2 Peter 2:4-9).

There are numerous things within this passage of Scripture that I will bring to your attention. The first specific thing I would like to point out is that this Old Testament occurrence is found in the New Testament. We can conclude from this that God has not changed. He is the same in the New Testament and Old Testament. His character and nature is constant. He is the same, yesterday, today, and forever (Hebrews 13:8).

Examples from Which to Learn

Paul declared that the things written in the Old Testament were written for our example. We are to learn from what took place in the lives of those who obeyed and those who disobeyed. We learn what to do and what not to do. We see the reward of both the righteous and the wicked.

Peter specifically says that these accounts of judgment in the Old Testament are an "example." We are able to peer into God's workings with man as we read what took place. We can observe God's character and nature even as we study how angels, cities, and individuals were judged and punished.

It's very interesting that Peter specifically mentions the two major judgments that take place in the Old Testament: the Great Flood and the Judgment of Sodom and Gomorrah. Peter says that these are an example to those who would live ungodly. In other words, this is a teaching on what will happen to the ungodly, not the righteous. This is the way that God deals with those who continue to reject the Lord and His commands.

Noah: Preacher and Builder

With that in mind, let's look at the account of Noah and the flood. This is a familiar story for most every Christian. This is something that is taught in kid's church and Sunday school classes around the world. Almost every kid's Sunday school class has placed a picture of Noah and the ark somewhere in their class at some time or another.

Noah is instructed of the Lord to build an ark. He is given specific dimensions to construct a ship that will be large enough to carry all kinds of animals along with provisions for his family. He is told that the Lord is going to destroy the entire earth along with every living thing in existence. Noah, being a righteous man, heeds the word of the Lord and obeys.

At the appropriate time, the animals that God elects to save are brought onto the ark. Then Noah and his family go into the ark. God shuts the door. It is not until God shuts the door that it begins to rain and eventually floods the earth.

There are several things that are not specifically mentioned in detail in the Bible about Noah. However, some research in the apocryphal ***Books of Jasher*** reveals that Noah preached repentance to the people for at least a hundred years before the flood. God gave the people an opportunity to change. He opened the door for people to be saved before the rain began to fall. They rejected salvation and reaped judgment.

Peter declares that Noah was a preacher of righteousness. We see the redemptive nature of God manifested in the fact that Noah was sent as an ambassador from heaven. God wanted to change their unrighteousness to righteousness. However, the people rejected the offer from heaven and chose rather to continue down the road of destruction.

God Saves the Righteous

With the fate of humanity sealed, God provides a means of safety and escape for Noah and his family. There is no flood until they are secure. There is no rain until God closes the door of the ark. Noah and his family are in the ark seven days BEFORE it began to rain (Genesis 7:10).

The principle I want you to observe at work here is that **God saves the righteous**. He separates them before judgment is released within the earth. The righteous are not partakers of the same experience. They are not destined to experience the wrath of God; they are destined for salvation.

God commanded Noah to build an ark to preserve the righteous. He saves Noah and his entire family along with the animals that He commanded Noah to take into the ark. God uses a floating zoo to preserve the life of Noah and his family. Although every living thing on earth was subject to the punishment, Noah and those with him were safe and unharmed.

God is Consistent

This is the example of which Peter speaks that we are to derive understanding. The way that God deals with Noah and the people of the earth are an example of what God will still do today. That's why I can emphatically say that God is not sending hurricanes and other storms to bring judgment because there are righteous people living in those regions being affected by these storms.

Again, this is inconsistent with the character and nature of God for Him to harm the righteous while punishing the wicked. The Bible reveals this is not the manner that God deals with man. That's NOT MY FATHER!

We see biblically that when there are judgments poured out, that God removes the righteous. The redeemed of the Lord are not in the middle of the bullseye. We are not the ones who are to suffer because of the idiotic behavior of people who are not saved. We are not the ones ordained to bear the punishment of the unbeliever.

After the waters recede, God makes covenant with Noah:

> Then Noah built an altar to the LORD, and took of every clean animal and of every clean bird, and offered burnt offerings on the altar. And the LORD smelled a soothing aroma. Then the LORD said in His heart, "I will never again curse the ground for man's sake, although the imagination of man's heart is evil from his youth; nor will I again destroy every living thing as I have done. "While the earth remains, Seedtime and harvest, Cold and heat, Winter and summer, And day and night Shall not cease" (Genesis 8:20-22).

Never Means Never

Within the covenant that God declares with Noah, God promises to never again curse the ground (earth) because of man's behavior. Along with that, He promises to never again destroy every living thing as He did in the flood.

Those statements alone should help us understand that God is NOT sending storms, hurricanes, tornados and other destructive forces to destroy the people of the earth. He promised that He would NEVER do that again. Can we believe what God said? I say an emphatic, "Yes!" Let God be true and every man a liar (Romans 3:4).

After declaring to Noah that He would never destroy the earth by flood, He begins talking about what will happen. God declares there will be seasons, and He also says that there will be seedtime and harvest.

Seasons Mean Weather

So, on the heels of a great judgment being poured out, God has some very important things to proclaim. He says that seasons are going to happen on the earth. Along with seasons comes seasonal weather. Some of that weather can be characterized by stormy occurrences.

When you combine all that the Lord declared, you realize He was saying there were going to be some storms. However, He would not send any to destroy the earth. God declared He would not destroy the earth by sending severe weather. I trust you are seeing this.

The weather we experience is a byproduct of the region in which we live and the seasons. So, hurricanes and tornados are not judgments from God; they are inherent in the weather patterns of the seasons where we live. They are a natural weather occurrence that take place in a fallen world.

Sowing and Reaping

It's interesting to note that God initiates the law of sowing and reaping in this passage of Scripture. This is not a law restricted for the natural realm only. It carries over into every realm of life. Some call it the law of reciprocation. This is a law that is repeated and articulated by both Jesus and Paul.

Jesus said with the same measure that you give, it will be given back to you. Paul said that God is not mocked and that whatever a man sows, he will also reap. This biblical principle is reemphasized throughout many New Testament Scriptures.

As I meditated on this, the Lord revealed something to me. God was making a declaration there would be no cataclysmic judgment that would come upon the earth. Rather, the way someone lives their life would be a seed that produces a harvest. The kind of harvest would be determined by the kind of seed sown. Paul said it this way:

> Do not be deceived, God is not mocked; for whatever a man sows, that he will also reap. For he who sows to his flesh will of the flesh reap corruption, but he who sows to the Spirit will of the Spirit reap everlasting life (Galatians 6:7-8).

Paul said that corruption would be the harvest in the life of someone who sowed to the flesh. The word "corruption" literally means ruin. Those who live in the flesh with sin and wickedness at the helm will reap the error of their way. The judgment they receive on earth is the harvest of the seed they sow; it is ruin and destruction. God need not pour out any judgment on those who practice wickedness on earth because God's spiritual law in place will cause them to be destroyed by their own sin. God doesn't send it; it happens because of a spiritual law.

Here's another Scripture that declares this principle:

> For this reason God gave them up to vile passions. For even their women exchanged the

> natural use for what is against nature. Likewise also the men, leaving the natural use of the woman, burned in their lust for one another, men with men committing what is shameful, and receiving in themselves the penalty of their error which was due (Romans 1:26-27).

It says in this Scripture that they receive "in themselves the penalty of their error." It doesn't say that everyone else receives the penalty or punishment. It declares that the one who sows the seed will reap the harvest. The seeds of sin sown in an individual's life will cause them to reap the harvest of destruction and ruin. However, the seeds of obedience sown in one's life will cause them to reap the harvest of life and blessing.

We must understand that God is not searching for a way or an excuse to release judgment. That's the reason we are exhorted in the Bible to walk in the Spirit and obey His commands. Why are we exhorted to do this? It is because God does not want us to experience ruin, destruction, and calamity. These are the things that sin produces. God desires for us to experience His life and blessing!

CHAPTER 9

SODOM AND GOMORRAH

For if God did not spare the angels who sinned, but cast them down to hell and delivered them into chains of darkness, to be reserved for judgment; and did not spare the ancient world, but saved Noah, one of eight people, a preacher of righteousness, bringing in the flood on the world of the ungodly; and turning the cities of Sodom and Gomorrah into ashes, condemned them to destruction, making them an example to those who afterward would live ungodly; and delivered righteous Lot, who was oppressed by the filthy conduct of the wicked (for that righteous man, dwelling among them, tormented his righteous soul from day to day by seeing and hearing their lawless deeds)—then the Lord knows how to deliver the godly out of temptations and to reserve the unjust under punishment for the day of judgment (2 Peter 2:4-9).

I want to bring this passage of Scripture back to your attention as we begin to discuss the judgment of Sodom and Gomorrah. Once again, Peter declares that this is written as an example of what happens to the ungodly. Sodom and Gomorrah is a picture of the punishment of the wicked who practice sinful deeds.

There have been many who have stated different opinions as to why God judged Sodom. Many have said it was because of the sexual perversion that was prevalent in the city, particularly that of homosexuality. Some have said it was the degree of sin in general that proliferated the territory. I personally believe that it was both. What we do know for sure is that the wickedness of the city was great.

Do Not Forget

It's interesting to note that Jesus mentions Sodom in relationship to judgment in Matthew 10:15. Peter mentions it in the previous Scripture as an example. Jude brings attention to Sodom in his epistle. Then John writes of Sodom in the book of Revelation. There are also numerous prophets in the Old Testament that specifically mention Sodom as they prophesy the word of the Lord.

The judgment of Sodom and Gomorrah is obviously something that God does not want us to forget. It is a story that is rehearsed throughout the Bible as a warning to those who would go down the same path of destruction. It is not mentioned to promote fear in the believer. Rather, it is mentioned to promote praise and thanksgiving for our deliverance from judgment. It is also repeated to induce a holy reverential fear of the Lord.

Since it is mentioned so many times in the Bible, it would benefit us to know exactly what took place. So, let's read the Scripture to find out. We pick up the story where God declares that He will not hide anything from Abraham. God reveals to Abraham His plan to destroy the cities of Sodom and Gomorrah.

> And the LORD said, "Because the outcry against Sodom and Gomorrah is great, and because their sin is very grave, I will go down now and see whether they have done altogether according to the outcry against it that has come to Me; and if not, I will know." Then the men turned away from there and went toward Sodom, but Abraham still stood before the LORD. And Abraham came near and said, "Would You also destroy the righteous with the wicked? Suppose there were fifty righteous within the city; would You also destroy the place and not spare it for the fifty righteous that were in it? Far be it from You to do such a thing as this, to slay the righteous with the wicked, so that the righteous should be as the wicked; far be it from You! Shall not the Judge of all the earth do right?" So the LORD said, "If I find in Sodom fifty righteous within the city, then *I will spare all the place for their sakes.*" Then Abraham answered and said, "Indeed now, I who am but dust and ashes have taken it upon myself to speak to the Lord: Suppose there were five less than the fifty righteous; would You destroy all of the city for lack of five?" So He said, "If I find there forty-five, *I*

> *will not destroy it.*" And he spoke to Him yet again and said, "Suppose there should be forty found there?" So He said, "*I will not do it for the sake of forty.*" Then he said, "Let not the Lord be angry, and I will speak: Suppose thirty should be found there?" So He said, "*I will not do it if I find thirty there.*" And he said, "Indeed now, I have taken it upon myself to speak to the Lord: Suppose twenty should be found there?" So He said, "*I will not destroy it for the sake of twenty.*" Then he said, "Let not the Lord be angry, and I will speak but once more: Suppose ten should be found there?" And He said, "*I will not destroy it for the sake of ten.*"So the LORD went His way as soon as He had finished speaking with Abraham; and Abraham returned to his place (Genesis 18:20-33, *emphasis mine*).

I Will Not Destroy It for Their Sake

Notice how many times God says, "I will not destroy it for their sake." Whose sake would God not destroy the city? For the sake of the righteous He would not do it! Every time Abraham asked the Lord if He would spare the city for the sake of the righteous, God answered that He would spare it.

Abraham asks God a question at the beginning of the narrative. In verse twenty-three he asks the Lord, "Would you also destroy the righteous with the wicked?" Then Abraham says this, "Far be it from You to do such a thing as this, to slay the righteous with the wicked; far be it from You! Shall not the Judge of all the earth do right?"

There is no indication that God corrects Abraham in his initial questioning or the assumptions he makes. All indications are that God agrees with Abraham. God declares that He will not destroy the city if there are righteous people there. Period! Here is the principle: **Righteousness is greater than judgment.**

Mercy and Salvation

Many times, we focus on the aspect of the judgment that rains down on Sodom. We talk about the punishment for their sin. However, we seem to miss God's hand of mercy that He extends continually throughout the entire narrative with Abraham. This mercy eventually involves the deliverance of Lot and his family. Peter talks about the salvation that Lot experienced (more details to follow).

Some have believed if Abraham had asked the Lord to spare the city for only one righteous person, God would have spared the entire city. I do not want to make that assumption; however, we do know that Peter said that Sodom vexed the soul of Lot. So, we would have to conclude that Lot needed to move from a city ridden with such great sin and wickedness. It was obviously having a negative effect on him and his family.

When I read this part of the account of Sodom and Gomorrah, it gives me insight to the character and nature of God. I see a Father who desires to extend mercy. He is looking for opportunity to spare the city. God was looking for the existence of some righteous people so that judgment could be averted. The Father didn't have a disposition toward the city whereby He was determined to destroy it and nothing could stop Him from doing it. He permitted Abraham to intercede on behalf of the city while He agreed with the conditions that Abraham placed upon mercy being granted.

This should really bring understanding to our hearts of the importance of intercessors. God looks for those who will stand in the gap. He looks for those who will cry for mercy where sin is in abundance. His eyes are moving throughout the earth looking for someone who will be like Abraham and intercede for the land.

After the angels of the Lord arrive in the city of Sodom, they go to Lot's house. They inform Lot that God plans to destroy the city of Sodom along with the cities throughout the region.

> Then the men said to Lot, "Have you anyone else here? Son-in-law, your sons, your daughters, and whomever you have in the city—take them out of this place! For we will destroy this place, because the outcry against them has grown great before the face of the LORD, and the LORD has sent us to destroy it." So Lot went out and spoke to his sons-in-law, who had married his daughters, and said, "Get up, get out of this place; for the LORD will destroy this city!" But to his sons-in-law he seemed to be joking. When the morning dawned, the angels urged Lot to hurry, saying, "Arise, take your wife and your two daughters who are here, lest you be consumed in the punishment of the city." And while he lingered,

the men took hold of his hand, his wife's hand, and the hands of his two daughters, the LORD being merciful to him, and they brought him out and set him outside the city. So it came to pass, when they had brought them outside, that he said, "Escape for your life! Do not look behind you nor stay anywhere in the plain. Escape to the mountains, lest you be destroyed." Then Lot said to them, "Please, no, my lords! Indeed now, your servant has found favor in your sight, and you have increased your mercy which you have shown me by saving my life; but I cannot escape to the mountains, lest some evil overtake me and I die. See now, this city is near enough to flee to, and it is a little one; please let me escape there (is it not a little one?) and my soul shall live." And he said to him, "See, I have favored you concerning this thing also, in that I will not overthrow this city for which you have spoken. Hurry, escape there. For I cannot do anything until you arrive there." Therefore the name of the city was called Zoar. The sun had risen upon the earth when Lot entered Zoar. Then the LORD rained brimstone and fire on Sodom and Gomorrah, from the LORD out of the heavens. So He overthrew those cities, all the plain, all the inhabitants of the cities, and what grew on the ground. And it came to pass, when God destroyed the cities of the plain, that God remembered Abraham, and sent Lot out of the midst of the overthrow, when He overthrew the cities in which Lot had dwelt (Genesis 19:12-25, 29).

Peter's narrative of this story is that God "delivered righteous Lot." Abraham interceded on behalf of the righteous, and God responded by rescuing Lot. If you look back at the beginning of Abraham's conversation with the Lord, it involves God not destroying the righteous with the wicked. God agrees with Abraham and does not destroy the city until the righteous are safe.

God Knows How to Deliver

There are many things to point out in this historical account of Sodom and Gomorrah. It is important that we see that this is an example of how God works. It reveals biblical principle that is consistent, unchanging, and at work. This is what Peter said. It is an example of how God deals with man. It is an example of how God delivers and saves the righteous.

We must understand this principle: **God will deliver the righteous from judgment.** The first thing we see as the angels of the Lord come into the city of Sodom is that they deliver a message to Lot. That message is that God will destroy the city. So, Lot and his family must leave immediately.

Peter said, "The Lord knows how to deliver the righteous." He spoke this regarding the account of Lot leaving Sodom. God sent angels to escort Lot and his family out to ensure his protection and safety. The Bible actually says that the Lord was merciful to Lot (Genesis 19:16). His mercy was demonstrated when the angels took him and his wife by the hand and escorted them outside the city.

When they arrived outside the walls, Lot was told to flee to the mountains. Lot replied that he was afraid that some kind of evil might happen to him. He requested that he be permitted to flee to the city of Zoar. This city was one that was to be destroyed along with Sodom. However, the angels said this, "I will not overthrow the city for which you have spoken."

The Petitions of the Righteous Abate Judgment

Here is another principle that we see demonstrated: **the *petitions* of the righteous will abate judgment.** An entire city was spared because Lot needed somewhere to stay overnight. All Lot did was make a request. That petition was granted, and God spared the city of Zoar. The Bible declares that the effectual fervent prayer of a righteous man avails much.

You will find that Lot did not remain in the city of Zoar and left immediately after God's judgment was poured out on Sodom. God spared an entire city solely because Lot needed a temporary stay. That is an amazing thing to consider. A city that was destined to be destroyed was spared because of the petition of a righteous man for an overnight stay. Think about it.

Nothing Can Happen Until...

After Lot's petition was granted, the angel told Lot to hurry. He went on to say, "For I cannot do anything until you arrive there." No judgment could be poured out on Sodom until Lot was safe in Zoar. Also, Zoar could not be saved until Lot arrived there. God's judgment was suspended until Lot and his family arrived in Zoar.

I want you to notice that the angel said, "I cannot." He didn't say that he wouldn't, but rather that he couldn't. Everything was in a place of suspension until Lot arrived and was safe. The angel could not do anything. God would not destroy the righteous with the wicked.

The Power of Presence

We see another principle demonstrated: **the *presence* of the righteous will abate judgment.** It is amazing for me to fathom that our presence in an area or region protects that territory. Why? It is because the presence of the righteous suspends and abates deserved judgment. Yes, your presence has power and a rippling effect. Could it be because our presence is His presence? Since He lives inside us, wherever we are physically present is the place God resides. Wow!

The city of Zoar deserved judgment just like all the other cities that received it. However, Lot's petition and presence brought protection to the entire city. Lot was the salt of that city; he was the preserving agent. Likewise, we are the salt of the territories where we live. We are agents of preservation.

Lot's presence in Zoar saved the city. His absence in Sodom sealed their fate. Once Lot made his move, God made His.

Righteousness Repels Judgment

It is important that we understand that God will not destroy the righteous with the wicked and ungodly. The righteous are judgment repellants. Why is that? It is because when God looks at you, He sees you through the blood of Jesus. He observes that you are now righteous and justified by faith.

When Jesus hung on the cross, He took the judgment for sin. Once someone is saved, judgment for sin is already satisfied. Jesus was already punished for our sin. We are not in line for judgment or punishment since Jesus already bore them. My sin and your sin were judged on the cross. That is the power of the cross and the blood of Jesus.

God will not pour out judgment on the wicked and ungodly while there are righteous people living there. The righteous are the preserving factor for the land. God will spare the land because the righteous are there. If God would spare an entire city from judgment just for Lot who needed a stayover, God will surely save the cities that believers already inhabit.

If there is a disaster where the righteous are being hurt along with the wicked, God didn't do it. It is not a judgment from God. It is an unfortunate event that may be caused from a naturally occurring storm or disaster. However, it is not being sent from the Lord and God's fingerprint is not on it. That's NOT MY FATHER!

If the righteous are harmed in a natural disaster, it is not a judgment from God. Again, God will not harm the righteous to punish the wicked and ungodly. We see in both the account of the Great Flood with Noah and the judgment of Sodom that God provides haven and security for the godly.

He is a loving Father. He cares for His people. He will not send judgment on the earth for the righteous to be partakers. That's NOT MY FATHER.

CHAPTER 10

GOD'S RIGHTEOUS JUDGMENT

And do you think this, O man, you who judge those practicing such things, and doing the same, that you will escape the judgment of God? Or do you despise the riches of His goodness, forbearance, and longsuffering, not knowing that the goodness of God leads you to repentance? But in accordance with your hardness and your impenitent heart you are treasuring up for yourself wrath in the day of wrath and revelation of the righteous judgment of God, who "**will render to each one according to his deeds**": eternal life to those who by patient continuance in doing good seek for glory, honor, and immortality; but to those who are self-seeking and do not obey the truth, but obey unrighteousness—indignation and wrath, tribulation and anguish, on every soul of man who does evil, of the Jew first and also of

> the Greek; but glory, honor, and peace to everyone who works what is good, to the Jew first and also to the Greek. For there is no partiality with God (Romans 2:3-11, emphasis mine).

It seems as there are two extremes in the body of Christ today. There are those who want to scream "judgment" at every turn and then there are those who are altogether afraid of the word.

One of the first things we must realize as believers is that "judgment" is a biblical word; it is not a bad word. Nor is it a word we are to avoid. However, it is not a word that should be thrown at every storm and disaster that happens in the world.

There are some people who reach for the word "judgment" anytime there is a tragic event in the world. If it is a weather event, a weather pattern is at work within the climate of the region that is affected. It is the byproduct of living in a fallen world. If someone enters a place to shoot and kill people, it's because they are controlled by demons. God has nothing to do with either of these types of tragedies.

So, I believe it is important to find out what the Bible says concerning judgment. We need to also observe the places where it occurs in the Word of God because it serves as an example for us to derive biblical principle. This is what we have been sharing in this writing. We have observed the different occurrences of judgment that are specifically mentioned in the New Testament as examples for us.

Judgment Explained

All judgment in one way or another is the consequence of the actions of man. Judgment is consequential in nature. It is the result of sinful behavior and lifestyles. It does not necessarily mean that God is sending it, but rather that it is cause and effect. Sin is the cause and, judgment is the effect. Judgment is always the consequence of the seed of sin that is sown.

For years I have defined "judgment" in the New Testament as the sudden harvest of the seeds of sin and wickedness sown over a period of time. When someone decides they are going to repeatedly sow the seed of wickedness, they place themselves in the arena to receive corruption, destruction, and death. Let's examine this verse again.

> Do not be deceived, God is not mocked; for whatever a man sows, that he will also reap. For he who sows to his flesh will of the flesh reap corruption, but he who sows to the Spirit will of the Spirit reap everlasting life (Galatians 6:7-8).

Judgment happens because of the spiritual law of sowing and reaping. Regarding this law, Paul declared that God would not be mocked. God is mocked if people practice wickedness without consequence. It proclaims that God's spiritual laws can be broken and there be no negative sanction. If people can practice evil and wickedness and then a harvest of destruction be circumvented, it would be a mockery to God. This is very important to understand.

According to Your Deeds

In the Scripture passage at the beginning of this chapter, Paul says that God "will render to each one according to his deeds." This is the judgment of God. Judgment is based upon the law of reciprocation or the law of sowing and reaping. Paul is very emphatic that the seeds of sin and fleshly behavior will ultimately reap a harvest of the righteous judgment of God. He also says that the seeds of righteous behavior (holy living) will reap eternal life.

I recognize that anytime you talk about works and rewards there are those who immediately want to say that you are going back to the Law. However, Paul is writing to New Testament believers in this passage of Scripture. He is declaring that the seeds sown through your behavior will determine what you receive. Why? It's because of the law of sowing and reaping.

When Paul speaks of the law of sowing and reaping in his letter to the Galatians, we should understand that he is writing to the church; he's not writing to the wicked. He says that God will not be mocked, and if you sow to the flesh, you will reap corruption. That's not law, it's New Testament principle.

Paul said that the wages of sin is death (Romans 6:23). In other words, sin and wickedness eventually have a payday. When people work for sin, it will be faithful to deliver its paycheck. It's not a paycheck of which anyone wants to be a recipient. However, the seed of sin and unrighteous deeds will deliver a payday.

Prophetic Judgments

Now, I want to share some things that involve what I call New Testament prophetic judgments. These are things that we see written in the book of Acts. The book of Acts is the text book for the way the church is to function today. It contains the historic account of the origins of the church and God's workings with His covenant people.

The most familiar prophetic judgment in the New Testament that we see is that of Ananias and Sapphira.

> But a certain man named Ananias, with Sapphira his wife, sold a possession. And he kept back part of the proceeds, his wife also being aware of it, and brought a certain part and laid it at the apostles' feet. But Peter said, "Ananias, why has Satan filled your heart to lie to the Holy Spirit and keep back part of the price of the land for yourself? While it remained, was it not your own? And after it was sold, was it not in your own control? Why have you conceived this thing in your heart? You have not lied to men but to God." Then Ananias, hearing these words, fell down and breathed his last. So great fear came upon all those who heard these things. And the young men arose and wrapped him up, carried him out, and buried him. Now it was about three hours later when his wife came in, not knowing what had happened. And Peter answered her, "Tell me whether you sold the land for so much?" She said, "Yes, for so much." Then

> Peter said to her, "How is it that you have agreed together to test the Spirit of the Lord? Look, the feet of those who have buried your husband are at the door, and they will carry you out." Then immediately she fell down at his feet and breathed her last. And the young men came in and found her dead, and carrying her out, buried her by her husband. So great fear came upon all the church and upon all who heard these things (Acts 5:1-11).

Looking at this at face value will cause you to scratch your head. It appears that Ananias and Sapphira didn't give enough in the offering and died as a result. However, it is much more than that; they lied to the Holy Spirit.

The Christianity demonstrated in the early church is something of which most believers are unfamiliar. The American church today has a difficult time wrapping its mind around many of the things that took place in the early church. Some may relish in it, but most look at it from a distance in bewilderment.

Ananias and Sapphira were a part of the church in Jerusalem. Some have said they were false believers. However, there is no indication that they were not saved. It is possible that they were like the "false brethren" that Paul talked about in Galatians 2:4. Perhaps they were spiritual wolves (Acts 20:29). Regardless of their spiritual condition, we know that they lied to the Holy Spirit. We know that they held back what they should have given. We know they sinned in a way that was grievous.

The Conspiracy Penalty

When Peter confronted Ananias with the truth, he died on the spot. His wife was given an opportunity to repent. However, she continued in the lie. She was asked if they sold the property for a certain price. She lied straight to Peter's face. Peter responded by telling her she had tested the Holy Spirit and that she would be carried out of the house, too.

They had conspired together; they lied to the Holy Spirit by lying to the leadership of the church. The Greek word that is translated "kept back" literally means to clandestinely embezzle. They secretly took for themselves what belonged to God. Wow! This was not a smart move.

The death of Ananias and Sapphira is what I call a prophetic judgment. When Peter rebukes people and then they die, I would say they are experiencing the punishment for their deeds. This is judgment in every sense of the word. Someone asked, "Do you think they went to heaven?" My answer is, "I haven't been there yet, but you can attempt to look them up when you get there." I think sometimes we get distracted with these types of questions and miss the principles being conveyed in the account.

Personalized and Localized

This is the biblical principle that stands out in this account. Judgment is rendered on a personal and localized plane. There is no one else in the room that dies. Peter doesn't die nor anyone with him at the time. The pallbearers don't die even though they are in the vicinity. God does not punish the righteous with the wicked. That's NOT MY FATHER!

The only ones who die are those who sinned. The only ones who die are those who secretly embezzled the money. Judgment affected those who were in the wrong, not those who were doing right. The righteous are protected when judgment is rendered.

God didn't send a horrendous storm on Jerusalem to judge the church because of the sin of one man and his wife. There were no earthquakes that hit the region because God was upset about the embezzlement that took place. God's judgment was only experienced by the ones who sinned: Ananias and Sapphira. They sowed to the flesh and then reaped corruption.

The good news is that on the other side of this occurrence, great fear comes upon the church. People stand up and take note that they should not be guilty of the same offense. We also see in the following verses of Scripture that the apostles do great signs and wonders, and there is unity within the church.

Not Appointed to Wrath

It is important to note that as believers, we are not ordained to reap the wrath or punishment of God.

> "For God did not appoint us to wrath, but to obtain salvation through our Lord Jesus Christ" (1 Thessalonians 5:9).

God has not appointed us to receive punishment. Judgment is never meant for the righteous. We must understand in the account of Ananias and Sapphira that they knew what they were doing, and it was premeditated. There is a big difference between a believer making a mistake versus a deliberate premeditated act of sin that involves lying to the Holy Spirit. They attempted to deceive the Lord and the apostolic leadership of the church.

Ananias and Sapphira reaped the harvest of the error of their conduct. They sowed the seed of sin and reaped the harvest of death. They received "in themselves the penalty of their error which was due" (Romans 1:27).

God is not mocked, for whatever a man sows, that will he also reap. That Scripture says that what a man sows, that will he also reap. It doesn't say: what a man sows, that will everybody in his city reap.

If a farmer plants seed in his field, he reaps and harvests in his own field. He doesn't go to another field across the street to harvest the fruit of the seed he planted in his field. If he plants them in his field, he harvests them in his field. **Harvest will always come in the field where seed is planted.**

Again, the judgment reaped in the life of the unrighteous is because of the seed they've planted in their own field. I am not the recipient of their harvest. Neither are you the recipient of their harvest. God is not holding the righteous accountable for the conduct of the wicked and ungodly. You should shout because of that!

> Now when they had gone through the island to Paphos, they found a certain sorcerer, a false prophet, a Jew whose name was Bar-Jesus, who was with the proconsul, Sergius Paulus, an intelligent man. This man called for Barnabas and Saul and sought to hear the word of God. But Elymas the sorcerer (for so his name is translated) withstood them, seeking to turn the proconsul away from the faith. Then Saul, who also is called Paul, filled with the Holy Spirit, looked intently at him and said, "O full of all deceit and all fraud, you son of the devil, you enemy of all righteousness, will you not cease perverting the straight ways of the Lord? And now, indeed, the hand of the Lord is upon you, and you shall be blind, not seeing the sun for a time." And immediately a dark mist fell on him, and he went around seeking someone to lead him by the hand. Then the proconsul believed, when he saw what had been done, being astonished at the teaching of the Lord (Acts 13:6-12).

Once again, we see a prophetic judgment being decreed over a man who is practicing sin. Bar-Jesus was a sorcerer and false prophet; he practiced witchcraft. This man attempted to withstand Paul from ministering to the proconsul. Bar-Jesus was endeavoring to turn the proconsul from the faith.

Understand that this man, Bar-Jesus, did not start practicing witchcraft the day before Paul arrived. This was something that he had practiced for years. He made his living practicing sorcery. It was his profession. He was an unrepentant man and was attempting to hurt those who were desirous of hearing the gospel. He was an evil man.

Inspired by the Holy Spirit

The account of this story specifically declares, "Paul, filled with the Holy Spirit, looked intently at him and said." The Scripture points out that Paul is filled with the Holy Spirit at the time he makes the declaration over Bar-Jesus. I believe we can say that Paul prophesied to Bar-Jesus. Paul didn't merely get upset and angry at him and then fly off the handle. Paul was moved by the Holy Spirit in everything he did and said. He spoke under the inspiration and anointing of the Holy Spirit.

So, Paul decrees a prophetic judgment over Bar-Jesus. He looks Bar-Jesus square in the eyes and says that the man is a deceitful, wicked, fraudulent son of the devil and enemy of righteousness. He furthermore says that Bar-Jesus is a pervert who distorts the way of the Lord. Wow!

Can you imagine a pastor or preacher saying that to someone today? He would be considered harsh and unloving. He would be talked about as uncaring and unmerciful. However, that's what Paul said. The actions of Bar-Jesus had surpassed the threshold of mercy and crossed over into the territory of judgment. He had moved beyond the place of sowing the seeds of wickedness into the place of reaping the harvest of judgment and destruction.

Paul continued to speak to Bar-Jesus and told him that the hand of the Lord was on him and that he would be blind. Immediately, Bar-Jesus lost his sight as a dark mist fell on him. The Bible goes on to say that then the proconsul believed. So, even in the pronouncing of a prophetic judgment, there was something redemptive that was born out of it.

It's Personal

Once again, we see how judgment in the New Testament is both personal and localized. Everyone standing near Bar-Jesus did not lose their sight. No one was affected by Paul's proclamation other than Bar-Jesus. No one else had to have someone lead them away by the hand. Bar-Jesus received the penalty of his error which was due! God used this incident to bring the proconsul to a place of repentance and belief in the Lord.

There are numerous other accounts throughout the Bible where we see this principle of judgment being personal and localized. When Pharaoh chased the Israelites after they had crossed the Red Sea, it was only the Egyptians (the wicked) that were drowned. All the Israelites were saved while the Egyptian army along with Pharaoh perished. Pharaoh sowed the seed of oppression and hatred and reaped the harvest of destruction.

Mercy and Love Always at Work

We must understand that when there is a judgment that God renders, there is still the element of love and mercy at work. It was God's mercy and love for Moses and the children of Israel that caused God to drown the Egyptian army. It was God's love for Abraham and Lot that caused judgment to come upon Sodom. However, His love manifests in the protection and safety of the righteous while the wicked and stiff-necked perish. His judgment on the wicked is His mercy manifested toward the righteous.

I personally believe that before judgment is ever released, God sends an opportunity for redemption and salvation. God gives fair warning to those who are on the path of condemnation and destruction. If someone slips and makes a mistake, God doesn't respond with wrath and indignation. That's NOT MY FATHER!

God is not looking for opportunity to pour out judgment, but rather to extend mercy and grace. He is not a grumpy old angry man who sits in heaven waiting for the smallest opportunity to punish someone. This is totally contrary to everything that Jesus said and demonstrated. He's not rubbing his hands together while saying, "I just can't wait to zap somebody." That's NOT MY FATHER!

God is not using storms and disasters to bring judgment upon the earth. Why? It is because the righteous are living there too! He is not anticipating the release of judgment, but rather the manifestation of redemption within the lives of people who will believe. He is a good God, and He is good all the time!

CHAPTER 11

GOOD GOD

"Oh, taste and see that the LORD is good; Blessed is the man who trusts in Him!" (Psalm 34:8).

One of the most basic, fundamental, and foundational understandings that we should possess as believers is that the Lord is good. It must be active within our lives. We must be rooted and grounded in this truth. It must be the lens through which we look at Scripture. Those who do not possess this understanding will perceive judgment incorrectly. Their perception of things will be riddled with error if this foundational truth is not seated well within their thinking.

The Psalmist said to "taste and see." The word "taste" means to perceive. Another way of saying this is that your perception of things should be filtered through the reality that the Lord is good. Those whose perception is filtered through the lens of the Lord as an angry God who wants to judge people, will see things incorrectly. It will result in them becoming angry, bitter, resentful, and judgmental. Their image of God will be reflected in their own lives.

Keep Your Lens Clean

There are those who wear corrective lens to be able to see properly. They must clean their glasses regularly so that their vision does not become clouded. If their glasses aren't clean, their vision is impaired. If contaminants are clinging to the lens, their perception will be distorted.

Likewise, if we don't look at things through the clean lens of God's goodness, we will have distorted vision. The constant revelation of the goodness of God will act as a lens cleaner within our lives. It will keep us from becoming judgmental and harsh. It will prevent bitterness and anger from taking hold of our lives.

The understanding that God is good causes you to be good. The revelation of His mercy will cause you to be merciful. Knowing His holiness will cause you to live holy. I trust you get the picture. Your lens determines what you see and perceive. It also determines what you reflect. We must perceive things through the understanding that the Lord is good!

The Common Thread of Goodness

Any study of the Bible will cause you to say that He is a good God. It is impossible for someone to study the Word of God and truthfully go away saying that God is bad. His goodness is revealed from the beginning of the book of Genesis until the end of the book of Revelation. God's goodness is a common thread that runs throughout the entire Bible.

After man sins in the garden and commits treason against God, the remaining narrative is all about redeeming man and placing him back into the position from which Adam fell. The Bible tells the story of God's love toward sinful man and His good will to see man restored.

When the angels appeared to the shepherds to announce the birth of Jesus, they declared, "Peace on earth, good will toward men." They didn't proclaim, "Oh you did it, now you're gonna' get it." It was the good will of a good God that they were proclaiming.

Think for a moment of where you are today and where you could have been. Today, I am saved rather than lost and dying in sin. I am healed rather than sick and hospitalized. I am alive rather than dead. My needs are met rather than living in poverty. I am more than a conqueror rather than a victim of circumstances. I serve a good God.

The Psalmist said, "Blessed is the man who trusts in Him." Well, who is Him? Him is the good God. Blessed is the man who puts his trust in the Lord who is good. Blessing comes on the heels of trusting in the Lord who is good. Blessing comes because we trust in His goodness.

Blessing is predicated on the revelation that the Lord is good. This one revelation and understanding has a dramatic affect in the lives of believers. It is the lens that causes us to see correctly.

Proper Aligned Thinking and Believing

The understanding that the Lord is a good God will properly align your thinking and believing. When automobile tires are out of alignment, it can cause numerous problems. One of the issues this creates is the car will not drive straight. It may pull to the left or the right. The driver may have to fight with the car to keep it in the middle of the lane. The tires will also wear improperly. The owner will be forced to purchase tires prematurely, and it will cost them.

There are Christians today who function with improper thinking and believing. They are out of alignment. It causes the car of their lives to pull to one side or the other. They become extreme in certain areas of their beliefs because their car keeps pulling them in that direction. They ultimately experience loss in their lives because they are out of alignment. The foundational understanding that the Lord is good will help you stay in spiritual alignment.

Eyes of Judgment or Eyes of Goodness?

There are those today who view everything through the lens of judgment. They have judgmental eyes. Their worldview is that God wants to zap everybody because the sin is so great. However, this is just not true.

Think about this for a moment. There were prophecies for years that God would send the Messiah. He would come to establish His kingdom and save all of Israel. So, in the fullness of time, the Father sends Jesus to the earth. He sends Him to be the Redeemer of mankind. He sends Him as the spotless Lamb slain from the foundation of the world. He sends Jesus to give His life as a ransom for many. But here is the kicker: He came to die for sinners.

When does all of this happen? It happens at a time when the Roman Empire is in its heyday. Sin and wickedness abound everywhere. There is sexual promiscuity at every turn; there is thievery and lying. There is slavery and murder. Anywhere and everywhere you look there is barbarism in manifestation. Wickedness is in full bloom.

What does the Father do at this time? He sends Jesus! He doesn't send judgment. He sends Jesus to take the judgment. He doesn't send punishment. He sends His only begotten Son to take the punishment for the sin of all humanity.

Why does He do this at this time? He does it because He is good! His love is so great that we cannot fathom it. It seems that at this time in history, judgment would be the appropriate rendering. However, He sends mercy and grace. It appears that destruction would be the order of the day, but instead He sends salvation.

God looks through eyes of love and mercy. Why? It is because He is a good God. If He looks through the eyes of goodness toward man, should we not do the same? We need to see through His eyes.

Goodness and Severity

> Therefore consider the goodness and severity of God: on those who fell, severity; but toward you, goodness, if you continue in His goodness. Otherwise you also will be cut off (Romans 11:22).

We see in this Scripture that God possesses both goodness and severity. It is important that we understand them both. There is a righteous judgment of God which we have discussed. However, every severe storm and natural disaster in the world is not the manifestation of judgment. Neither is it the severity of God.

Paul brings to light that while God is good, there is an aspect of severity that we should not ignore. In the context of the Scripture, the goodness of God is revealed in the life of those who believe on Jesus. The severity of God is revealed in the lives of those who reject Jesus and refuse to believe on Him.

I think it's important to note in this Scripture that the exhortation is to "continue in His goodness." It's not "continue in His severity." Severity is the consequence of rejecting the Lord.

In the previous verse of Scripture, Paul declares the consequence of not continuing in the goodness of God is that one can be cut off. Now there are different ways that people can possibly interpret what it means to be cut off. Regardless of your interpretation, this is not a good thing. I don't want to be cut off, so I am going to continue in God's goodness!

Forfeiting Blessing

We must understand that God is not actually cutting people off through His severity. They cut themselves off through their unbelief and failure to submit to Him. Many people forfeit the blessing of God because they fail to continue in God's goodness. They fail to believe that He is a good God.

Those who do not continue in the goodness of God ultimately forfeit blessing that God has ordained for them. They cut themselves off from God's best for their lives. Their failure to perceive through the eyes of God's goodness prevents the reception of blessing.

When people begin to look at everything through the lens of judgment and severity it causes negative consequences within their own lives. They begin to disconnect. They disconnect with the local church because there's no church that is doing it right. They find fault in everything that is happening in the church. You name it, it's wrong. Of course, they say, "Everyone is a hypocrite." When I hear someone say that, my response is, "Come join us, we could always use one more."

These kinds of people believe they have it altogether and that everyone else is spiritually ignorant. They walk around with the Elijah syndrome believing that they are the only ones who really have a heart after God. This kind of attitude and disposition usually stems from looking through the lens of judgment and fault-finding. My counsel to these people is to clean their glasses.

Those who look through the lens of judgment also live their lives without joy. They are usually the spiritual sourpusses. They disconnect from people within the church. The truth is that no one in the church really wants to be around them. They are the storm cloud in the middle of the sunshine. My recommendation to them is to clean their glasses.

Unity vs. Conformity

Another thing that I've noticed about people who view from the disposition of judgment is they have a condemning attitude toward others that are not just like them. They say they believe in unity, but really want to force conformity. This type of person will disconnect from those who are not EXACTLY like them. If others don't support the same political candidate that they have deemed to be the messenger from heaven, they will disconnect from them.

Remember the Scripture we shared that we must continue in God's goodness or be cut off. This is what is happening. Those who look through the lens of judgment cut themselves off or disconnect from people that are not exactly like them.

I believe that the lens of judgment keeps people from walking in the unity of the Spirit. Why? It is because they see everyone who does not conform to their exact way of thinking as their enemy. They see them as spiritually void. I've seen this manifest in people in the church. It is very unfortunate because they cut themselves off. They forfeit the blessing of God because of the lens they are looking through.

People Are Not the Enemy

It is important that we see the world through the lens of God's goodness and mercy. If we don't, we will view people as our enemies. People are not our enemy and neither are they God's enemy. God is not out to destroy people; He wants to save them. We must begin to see people through the lens of the goodness of God.

> For we do not wrestle against flesh and blood, but against principalities, against powers, against the rulers of the darkness of this age, against spiritual hosts of wickedness in the heavenly places (Ephesians 6:12).

Paul declares that our war is not with people. Our battle is with demonic forces that are at work in the world. These entities manifest their works through the lives of those they hold captive and have enslaved. We are called to liberate them from the hold of our enemy. These demonic entities are our enemy, not the people who are their captives.

It's only when you look through the lens of God's goodness that you can transcend the flesh barrier. Only then can you see beyond the veil of the flesh and see the enemy who is holding people in captivity. We are called to love the sinner and hate the sin. We are called to love the demonized by liberating them from the hold of satan. This is the goodness of God.

Figuring this out is fairly simple. Here is the measuring stick we use: **God is good, and the devil is bad.** It's just that simple; it's not complicated. God desires to pour out

His goodness in our lives. The devil desires to bring destruction and death. What do you want? I want the goodness of God!

> Now it came to pass, when the time had come for Him to be received up, that He steadfastly set His face to go to Jerusalem, and sent messengers before His face. And as they went, they entered a village of the Samaritans, to prepare for Him. But they did not receive Him, because His face was set for the journey to Jerusalem. And when His disciples James and John saw this, they said, "Lord, do You want us to command fire to come down from heaven and consume them, just as Elijah did?" But He turned and rebuked them, and said, "You do not know what manner of spirit you are of. For the Son of Man did not come to destroy men's lives but to save them." And they went to another village (Luke 9:51-56).

I believe that this is a very important Scripture for us to know. It gives us insight to the very heart of God. Jesus reveals God's character and nature. He reveals the heart of the Father God. We can see the goodness and mercy of God in manifestation.

Wrong Spirit

James and John wanted to command fire to come from heaven because the Samaritans rejected the Lord. They were upset and angry; they were indignant. They were insulted and offended. How could they reject the Son of God?

Then they attempted to use a biblical justification for decreeing judgment by using the phrase "just as Elijah did." They believed that they would be justified in commanding fire to come on them. They believed this was worthy of judgment. In the minds of the disciples, the Samaritans had messed with the bull and now they would get the horns. This was their attitude and disposition.

Jesus turns to them and REBUKES them. That's right. He rebuked the ones who had chosen to follow Him while defending the ones who rejected Him. Wow! Jesus doesn't commend His disciples for attempting to defend Him. He rebukes them because it was not the correct thing for them to do. This was not the righteous thing to do. It was not the godly course to take. The disciples needed to clean their glasses. The lens they were looking through had been contaminated.

Jesus then said, "You do not know what manner of spirit you are of." Let me paraphrase this for you. "Boys, you are not operating in the goodness of God, you are operating in the flesh." Jesus was letting them know that the lens they were looking through was the lens of judgment rather than the lens of goodness and mercy.

Jesus then said, "The Son of Man did not come to destroy men's lives but to save them." He was saying to James and John, "Guys, I didn't come to bring judgment and punishment. I came to deliver and save people from judgment."

The disciples were operating in the flesh. They were looking through the lens of judgment. Jesus said they were operating in the wrong spirit. He brought correction to them.

I believe the people who are quick to say "judgment" are operating in the wrong spirit. I am not saying they are evil, just like James and John were not evil. However, people who love God can still operate in the wrong spirit. They do this because they perceive things through the lens of judgment rather than God's goodness.

I've heard people say, "The sin is so bad in the world that God must send judgment." They say it is worse than it's ever been in the history of mankind. I would encourage them to study world history. There have been times in history where things took place that were far worse in magnitude. As hard as that may be to believe, it has happened.

Where Sin Abounds, Grace is Greater

Evil in the heart of man is not something new. It has been in existence for a long time. Sin is present in every city in America today; it is present throughout the world. However, where sin abounds, grace abounds greater. God's goodness is greater. God is not looking for a reason to render judgment, rather an opportunity to extend mercy, grace, and goodness.

For those who want to say that God is pouring out judgment in the United States today, I would reiterate the words of Jesus: He did not come to destroy, but to save. He came to "seek and to save that which was lost." Jesus came to restore man. He came to bring us back to the place from which Adam fell. He came to manifest God's goodness so that we could receive the fullness of His blessing.

We must look at the world through the lens of God's goodness. It will cause us to begin to see as He sees. It will align our perspective so that we can be effective in the kingdom of God. As we do, we will become agents of God's goodness and see freedom ministered to those who are bound.

God is good all the time. And all the time God is good! If it's not good, then it's NOT MY FATHER!

CHAPTER 12
FINAL THOUGHTS

> Therefore we make it our aim, whether present or absent, to be well pleasing to Him. For we must all appear before the judgment seat of Christ, that each one may receive the things done in the body, according to what he has done, whether good or bad (2 Corinthians 5:9-10).

There are many aspects of the judgment of God that we have not discussed within the pages of this book. We have not mentioned the Great White Throne Judgment that we see in the book of Revelation where the wicked will be judged and then cast into the lake of fire (Revelation 20:11-15). Also, we have not discussed the Judgment Seat of Christ that Paul speaks of where believers will give an account for the manner in which they conducted their lives (2 Corinthians 5:10). There, believers will be rewarded for what they did and how they lived. Both of these events take place after life, as we know it, ceases on the earth.

These future culminating happenings have been discussed in numerous books that have been written by different authors. It is recognized that there will be a day when we will give an account for our actions. It is agreed by most all theologians and Bible teachers that a time will come when everyone will stand before God and be judged. However, the focus of this book has been to bring to light the nature of the Father as it pertains to storms, disasters, and judgment in the earth today. We are not discussing the final judgment that will happen within the scope of eternity. It is important that we do not get the two confused with one another.

Executing Judgment

For many years, I was a worship leader and songwriter. During that time, I wrote many songs concerning the warrior nature of God. Some of the songs I wrote included lyrics pertaining to executing the judgment of God. The judgment that I wrote about in these songs related to satan and demonic forces. We, as the church, are called and commissioned to execute and enforce the written judgment upon the enemy (Psalm 149).

We are to use our authority in Christ to impose the victory of Jesus in the earth. There was a judgment pronounced in our favor through the death and resurrection of Jesus. That judgment is to be executed and enforced. The Father ruled in our favor as Jesus paid the price for our sin. We are to execute that judgment in the earth and upon the enemy of our soul.

This, in a similar manner, is a different aspect of judgment that is released through the high praises of God and His Word. This is a facet of judgment in which believers are involved and participate. However, people are not the target; the devil is the target.

It is important that we understand that judgment that is to be executed presently is designed for satan. It is not designed for the believer. It is not even designed for the unbeliever.

Separation and Scapegoat

As stated previously, God does not harm the righteous in order to punish or judge the wicked. He will not put His people in the same basket with unbelievers. We are sanctified and set apart. He has separated us from the those who are of the world. God loves His children and will not send any harmful judgment their direction.

> "For He made Him who knew no sin to be sin for us, that we might become the righteousness of God in Him" (2 Corinthians 5:21).

In the Old Testament, the high priest would lay his hands upon a goat to transfer the sin of the people. This scapegoat would be led into the wilderness where judgment would be passed. The focus of the judgment was not the goat, but rather the sin that the goat embodied. The scapegoat had taken the sin, and judgment was released upon that sin.

The scapegoat would be led into the wilderness alive and there be released. Therefore, the sin that the goat bore was separated from the people. Sin was distanced from them because the goat embodied it.

Jesus came as the Lamb of God. He also became the scapegoat in that He took upon Himself the sin of all humanity. In the same manner that judgment was enacted upon the scapegoat in Levitical Law, judgment was enacted upon Jesus as He hung on the cross and embodied the sin of mankind. He literally became sin for us.

Now, we who believe upon Him are the righteousness of God in Christ. What does that mean? It means that judgment has already been passed, and we are free! Jesus took the judgment so that we could receive salvation instead. It means that God CANNOT release judgment on you because it was already released on Jesus.

Double Jeopardy

In our legal system, there is a term called "double jeopardy." It means that a person cannot be tried for the same crime repeatedly. It's one and done. Once you stand trial for something and a judgment is rendered, you cannot be tried for that crime again.

This is great news for us because Jesus went to trial for your sin and my sin. Judgment was rendered on our sin through the substitutionary act that was carried out by Jesus at the cross. Since a verdict and judgment was rendered upon sin, there in no more punishment for that sin! That means NO JUDGMENT! Hallelujah!

While I know that God is not controlled by the legal systems of man, it would be a situation of double jeopardy if God sent judgment upon the righteous. The righteous would then be suffering for sin that was already judged at the cross. It would diminish the very power of the cross and everything that Jesus accomplished.

No More Pointing the Finger

The reality is that God is not sending storms and disasters to judge the earth. He is not the author of these events, and it's time for people to stop pointing the finger toward heaven when these things happen. That's NOT MY FATHER.

While there is a righteous judgment of God, He is not punishing His people for the sin of all humanity. Jesus already received that punishment. God is not looking for a reason or justification to send a disaster to certain regions of the world. He is not looking for opportunity to "zap" somebody. He is a good Father and loves His people and the world where they live.

His goodness and mercy are unceasing. His love is never ending. His grace reaches beyond the realms of our thinking. It is important that we use these understandings as the lens through which we view things. It is imperative that our spiritual filter is filled with the goodness of God.

As we view things from that perspective, we will see clearly. There will be a new outlook on life and the world around us. We will embrace the understanding of a Father who loves and cares for His people greater than a natural father loves his own children. We will then boldly say in the face of any storm, disaster, or person crying judgment, "THAT'S NOT MY FATHER!"

ABOUT THE AUTHOR

ROBERT GAY is Senior Pastor and Apostolic founder of High Praise Worship Center in Panama City, Florida. He and his wife Stacey were married in 1981 and today have three children who serve in ministry along with them. Their ministry has a three-fold vision statement: Equipping Believers, Building Families, and Furthering the Kingdom of God. Robert provides apostolic oversight to multiple High Praise churches within the United States. He is recognized by many as an Apostolic Father bringing balance and order into the church today. For complete bio go to www.highpraisepc.com.

Silencing The Enemy With Praise

Pastor Robert Gay

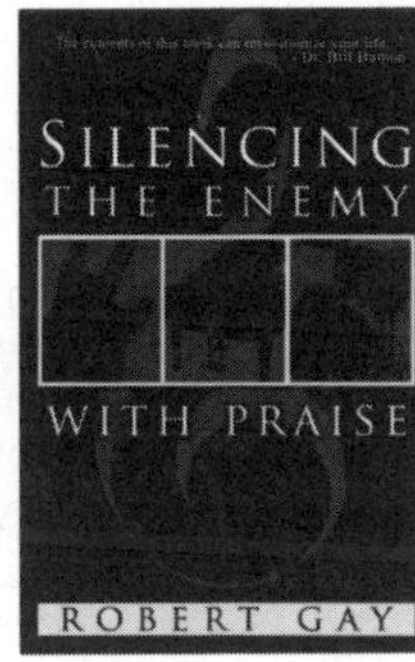

Praise and worship are more than words and music says author Pastor Robert Gay. Praise is a weapon of warfare. God will fight for you as you praise the greatness of His name.

"The contents of this book can revolutionize your life...It brings new understanding about the power of praise and worship."
-Dr. Bill Hamon

Planted

Pastor Robert Gay

Robert Gay confronts common "church issues" head on. He teaches with clarity and compassion that God is the Master Gardener who lovengly tends to every individual planted in His garden. You will find out how God wants to plant you so that you will flourish and grow and become everything He wants you to be.

"Every Pastor will appreciate this book...every saint of God should read this book..." - Dr. Bill Hamon

Best Of Robert Gay

Pastor Robert Gay

This compilation album represents some of Robert's most impactful songs that have touched the body of Christ throughout the world. This cd is packed full with 19 tracks that include powerful songs such as Mighty Man of War, Lord Sabaoth, On Bended Knee, Holy is Your Name, One Voice, No Other Name and much more!

HIGH PRAISE MEDIA PRODUCTS **for more products or to order any of these products visit our online store at**
WWW.HIGHPRAISEPC.COM/ONLINE-STORE

Sonship
Pastor Joshua Gay

Discover the life of a true son through study of the Scripture and powerful testimonies. The author shines the light on many pitfalls that ensnare today's generation while revealing the true picture of faithful spiritual sons and daughters.

"This book needs to be read by every person who wants to be a true son or father according to God's order." - Dr. Bill Hamon

Faith Force Academy LIVE DVD
Volume 1: Meet The Faith Force

Join the Faith Force Heroes and Professors M & C in *Faith Force Academy LIVE!* as they teach you how to become strong superheroes of faith! This volume contains 4 exciting episodes that kids of all ages will be sure to enjoy. Each episode features exciting praise & worship, step by step teaching of scripture memory verses, incredible life-sized characters, & illustrated sermons.

Faith Force Academy LIVE DVD
Volume 2: Faith Is The Victory

Join the Faith Force Heroes and Professors M & C in *Faith Force Academy LIVE!* as they teach you how faith is our victory! This volume contains 4 exciting episodes that kids of all ages will be sure to enjoy. Each episode features exciting praise & worship, step by step teaching of scripture memory verses, incredible life-sized characters, & illustrated sermons.

HIGH PRAISE MEDIA PRODUCTS for more products or to order any of these products visit our online store at **WWW.HIGHPRAISEPC.COM/ONLINE-STORE**

Jesus In 3D
Pastor Robert Gay

Do you want to express the life of God in every aspect of your life? In your ministry? For us to walk in the totality of Jesus, we must first cherish the fullness of His ministry. Every dimension of the ministry of Jesus is critical for us to have ultimate effectiveness for the kingdom of God. Today, if you want to reflect the life of God, you must receive and activate all that He did, everything He said, and everything He demonstrated.

Revolutionaires
Pastor Joshua Gay

Revolutionaries declares to readers that God is raising up a transformation generation in the earth today. Discover the life of a spiritual revolutionary through the study of scripture and parallels from history.

"...if you read this book you are going to be enlightened, motivated and activated into being one of God's "Revolutionaries." - Dr. Bill Hamon

Building Strong
Pastor Robert Gay

There is a blueprint that the Father has rendered for the design of the Church. Jesus has been given the responsibility of building what was in the mind of the Father from creation. The Holy Spirit is the agent that empowers and gifts the spiritual subcontractors here on earth to build according to the plan that has been rendered from heaven.

JESUS
IN 3D
LIVING IN THE FULLNESS OF GOD
ROBERT GAY
FOR BULK ORDER INFO AND PRICES
CALL (850) 874-9745

HIGHPRAISE
PANAMA CITY
SUN: 9AM & 11AM // WED: 7PM
CONNECT WITH US ONLINE @HIGHPRAISEPC
Instagram
HIGHPRAISEPC.COM
pastors
ROBERT & STACEY GAY
SCAN HERE FOR
MORE INFO ABOUT
HIGH PRAISE
PANAMA CITY

HIGHPRAISE
PODCAST
Search 'High Praise' in iTunes
subscribe and listen to many powerful messages by
Pastor Joshua Gay, Apostle Robert Gay & more
SCAN QR CODE TO GO TO
HIGH PRAISE
PODCASTS

GET SOCIAL WITH US

@HIGHPRAISEPC
@HIGHPRAISEORL